D1453691

FARMINGTON COMMUNITY LIBRARY

FARMINGTON FRIENDS OF THE LIBRARY

HONOR

LISA BROOKINS

FOR VOLUNTEER SERVICE

ROSES and Revolutions

wayne state university press   detroit

The Selected Writings of DUDLEY RANDALL

ROSES and Revolutions

Edited and with an Introduction by Melba Joyce Boyd

AFRICAN AMERICAN LIFE SERIES

*A complete listing of the books in this series
can be found online at wsupress.wayne.edu*

Series Editors

Melba Joyce Boyd
Department of Africana Studies, Wayne State University

Ronald Brown
Department of Political Science, Wayne State University

13 12 11 10 09   5 4 3 2 1

LIBRARY OF CONGRESS CATALOGING-IN-PUBLICATION DATA

RANDALL, DUDLEY, 1914–2000
[SELECTIONS. 2009]
ROSES AND REVOLUTIONS : THE SELECTED WRITINGS OF DUDLEY RANDALL /
EDITED AND WITH AN INTRODUCTION BY MELBA JOYCE BOYD.
P. CM. — (AFRICAN AMERICAN LIFE SERIES)
INCLUDES BIBLIOGRAPHICAL REFERENCES.
ISBN 978-0-8143-3445-4 (CLOTH : ALK. PAPER)
I. BOYD, MELBA JOYCE. II. TITLE.
PS3568.A49A6 2009
818'.5409—DC22
2008052805

*Designed and typeset by Maya Rhodes
Composed in Adobe Garamond Pro and Eccentric Std*

THIS BOOK IS DEDICATED TO DUDLEY'S DAUGHTER,

Phyllis Randall Sherron

CONTENTS

DIALECTICS OF THE BLACK AESTHETIC

Essay

Randall reading, 1975. (Photo by Kwado Akpan, courtesy of Laura Mosley Collection)

INTRODUCTION - MELBA JOYCE BOYD

When I was completing the manuscript for *Wrestling with the Muse: Dudley Randall and the Broadside Press,* Randall and I discussed the prospect of a book of his collected poems in order to ensure his literary longevity. He did not perceive the urgency that I projected on the subject, but at the time of his death, August 11, 2000, all of his poetry books were out of print. Permissions to reprint his poetry persist, and his most popular poems continue to survive in numerous anthologies. However, the absence of a comprehensive collection of Randall's writings leaves a void in his literary legacy and in the libraries. *Roses and Revolutions: The Selected Writings of Dudley Randall* represents the multidimensionality of his literary expressions—poetry, short fiction, and essays—in a single volume. This collection dispels current notions about the breadth of Randall's oeuvre and illustrates his passion, his wit, his craftsmanship, his unique perspective, and his cultural insight. These selected writings not only confirm the talent and the creative intellect of this preeminent African American author and editor but also demonstrate why his voice remains relevant and impressive in the twenty-first century.

The poem "Roses and Revolutions" provides an expansive theme that coincides and intersects with various planes of Randall's literary vision; therefore, it was the appropriate title for a collection of Randall's writings. In a 1971 interview, he commented on this poem and on political themes and artistic expression:

> I don't know whether you would call me a full-time revolutionary poet. I write about the struggle when I am moved to write about it. My poem "Roses and Revolutions," which I consider prophetic, was written as long

ago as 1948. But I don't consider this my whole expression. I would say, "Nothing human is alien to me," quoting the Roman African writer, Terence. I write about the whole gamut of human experience, which includes liberation. I don't believe, however, that the poet is programmatic. He may be programmatic in his outside life, but, in poetry, you cannot lay down a blueprint or a program for revolution. This is something which requires careful planning, organization, discipline, and hard, humdrum, routine work. I don't think that poetry should bore people by preaching to them. Being a preacher's son, I've heard too many sermons. I write poetry in order to move people—to give them the emotions and the ideas, which could perhaps lead to a better life. I also believe that poetry is something which gives pleasure—something which people enjoy.[1]

An assessment of Randall's writings reveals a devotion to a range of themes about various loves and revolutions. In this regard, love often emerges as a primary theme in poems with warlike settings. Concurrently, the civil rights movement to achieve racial equality constituted a domestic struggle within the United States that influenced Randall as an African American writer. In opposition to repressive racial policies and practices, disagreements between civil rights organizations evolved. Similarly, aesthetic arguments between writers resulted in cultural conflict during the Black Arts movement. Hence, many of Randall's poems assess conflicting loyalties, contradictory perspectives, and contrary circumstances.

But within this turmoil, Randall advocates the joy of life and the pleasure of poetry. He consistently exhibits life's complexities in geometric poetic constructions: parallels and opposites, comparisons and contrasts, point and counterpoint. Randall's poetry is reflexive and reflective, revealing elements and areas of intersection while providing a broader perspective for introspection. As in "Roses and Revolutions," contrary associations illustrate the dialectic and the resolution. This poem is both a love poem and a war poem; it is a poem about terror and about peace, about the past and about the future. Because of these overarching dimensions, I think that this poem best represents Randall's oeuvre and the broadest purpose for all of his writings. For these reasons and because of its literary distinction, "Roses and Revolutions" could be considered Randall's signature poem. It is also the theme that I believe best represents the heart of this definitive collection of writings by Dudley Randall.

26 Apr 48

MUSING ON ROSES AND SPRINGTIME

Musing on roses and springtime,
I saw night close down on the earth like the folding of a wing,
And the lights of cities were as tapers in the night,
And I heard the lamentations of a million hearts
Regretting life and crying for the grave.
I saw the Negro lying in the swamp with his face blown off,
Or in northern cities with his manhood maligned ~~maligned~~ and felt the
   writhing/Of his viscera
Like that of the hare hunted down or the bear at bay.
And I saw men working and taking no joy in their work
And embracing the hard~~ness of the~~ whore with joyless excitement
And with wives and virgins lying in impotence.

And as I felt the pain of millions
And groped with them in darkness,
Then, as day drives night across the continent,
I saw shining upon them the light of visions
Of a time when every man shall love his brother
And all men stand/~~erect~~ and walk ~~proudly~~ through the earth,
And the bombs and the battleships shall lie at the bottom of the ocean
Like the bones of dinosaurs buried under the shale of centuries,
And men shall strive with each other not for power or the accumulation
   of paper
But in joy shall create for others the house, the poem, the task of loving
   service.

Then enveloped in the bright atmosphere of this vision,
I saw how under its power would grow and be nourished and suddenly
Burst into terrible and splendid bloom
The blood-red flower of revolution.

"Musing on Roses and Springtime" is an early draft of the poem "Roses and Revolutions," dated April 26, 1948, when Randall was a student at Wayne State University. The title and several words and phrases were transformed in the final version.

Biographical Overview

Dudley Felker Randall was born on January 14, 1914, in Washington, D.C. The third of Rev. Arthur Randall and Ada Bradley Randall's five children, Dudley grew up in a middle-class home, where his college-educated parents instilled a belief in racial justice, promoted education, and encouraged an appreciation of poetry. The family library contained works by African American authors as well as world literatures in several languages. Consequently, Dudley Randall's literary development included an appreciation of African American literature within the broader context of world cultures.

Because of the widespread practice of racial segregation and discrimination against blacks, the Randalls moved to a number of cities in search of better employment opportunities. They finally settled in Detroit, Michigan, in 1920. As a consequence of his father's political activities and cultural affiliations, Dudley Randall met many prominent African Americans during his youth, including W. E. B. Du Bois and James Weldon Johnson. Randall read incessantly, studied several languages, and began writing poetry at the age of fourteen.

Randall graduated from Eastern High School in 1930 when he was only sixteen years old, but because of economic hardships that beset the Randall family during the Great Depression, he was unable to attend college. He began work in the blast furnace in the Ford Motor Company foundry when he was eighteen and joined the United Auto Workers. In 1935 he married the first of three wives, Ruby Hudson (divorced 1942), who became the mother of his only child, Phyllis. After Randall was laid off, he got a job as a postal carrier and was active in the Postal Carriers Union. Despite the delay of his college education and a dearth of publishing opportunities, his interest in poetry thrived. In 1937 he met Robert Hayden, and they forged a friendship through union activities and frequent meetings to share and critique their poetry.

In 1943 Randall married his second wife, Mildred Pinckney (divorced 1954); was drafted into a segregated U.S. Army; and served his duty in the South Pacific until the end of World War II. He returned to work at the U.S. Postal Service in Detroit, and in 1946 he enrolled in Wayne University (renamed Wayne State University in 1956), where he majored in English, studied Russian language and literature, pledged Kappa Alpha Psi Fraternity, and joined the Miles Modern Poetry Workshop. It was through the workshop's publication, *Milestones,* that Randall first published the poem "Roses and Revolutions" (1948).

In 1949 Randall entered the master's degree program in library science at the University of Michigan in Ann Arbor. After graduation in 1951 he became a librarian at Lincoln University in Jefferson, Missouri, where one of his more famous poems, "Booker T. and W. E. B.," was published in the university's *Midwest Journal* (Winter 1952–53). Randall left Lincoln University for a librarian position at Morgan State College in Baltimore, Maryland (1954–56), and eventually returned to Detroit in 1956 for a job with the Wayne County Federated Library System. That same year he met Vivian Spencer, a social worker, and on May 4, 1957, they were married.

In 1962 Randall enrolled in a master's degree program in humanities at Wayne State University. He never completed this degree, but in 1980 he composed the poem "Translation from Chopin (Prelude Number 7 in A Major, Opus 28)," which was derived from the premise for his thesis, to translate Chopin's sonatas into poetry. Randall also reconnected with the still-active Miles Modern Poetry Workshop; the poem "The Poet" is based on his perceptions of the Beat movement and the changing character of American poetry during that period. That same year he met Margaret Danner, a Chicago poet, who was a visiting professor at Wayne State University and founder of Boone House, a black writing community. Randall joined Boone House and developed lifelong friendships with many in the group, including poet Naomi Long Madgett and playwright Ron Milner.

As the civil rights movement was gaining the attention of the nation, a vital cultural renaissance was likewise emerging. Hoyt Fuller, who was a classmate of Randall's at Wayne State University, became the editor of the Chicago-based *Negro Digest* in 1962. Fuller frequently published Randall's poetry, prose, essays, and book reviews and consulted with him on editorial matters that shaped the development of this key intellectual and cultural periodical. During this time, Randall's writings also appeared in the *Negro History Bulletin, Free Lance, Correspondence,* and other leftist and progressive periodicals. His poetry gained national attention and international notice in the Detroit poetry anthology *Ten,* in Rosie Pool's anthologies *Beyond the Blues* and *Ik Ben de Nieuwe Neger* (I Am the New Negro), and in Langston Hughes's *New Negro Poets, USA.*

But Randall's most prominent civil rights poem, "Ballad of Birmingham," was published on the front page of the leftist publication *Correspondence* in its autumn 1963 issue.[2] According to James Smethhurst's comprehensive study, *The Black Arts Movement: Literary Nationalism in the 1960s and 1970s, Correspondence* developed a "Left nationalist stance under the auspices of Grace

25 cents

BALLAD OF BIRMINGHAM
(On the bombing of a church in Birmingham)
By Dudley Randall
"Mother dear, may I go downtown
    Instead of out to play,
And march the streets of Birmingham
    In the Freedom March today?"

"No, baby, no, you may not go,
    For the dogs are fierce and wild,
And clubs and hoses, guns and jails
    Aren't good for a little child."

"But, mother, I won't be alone.
    More children will go with me,
And march the streets of Birmingham
    To make our country free."

"No, baby, no, you may not go,
    For I fear those guns will fire.
But you may go to church instead,
    And sing in the children's choir."

She has combed and brushed her nightdark hair,
    And bathed rose petal sweet,
And drawn white gloves on her small brown hands,
    And white shoes on her feet.

The mother smiled to know her child
    Was in the sacred place,
But that smile was the last smile
    To come upon her face.

For when she heard the explosion,
    Her eyes grew wet and wild.
She raced through the streets of Birmingham
    Calling for her child.

She clawed in bits of glass and brick,
    Then lifted out a shoe.
"O, here's a shoe, but where's the foot,
    And, baby, where are you?"

© Copyright 1963 and 1965 Melody Trails, Inc. New York, N.Y.

Also available in the song, BALLAD OF BIRMINGHAM,
Words by Dudley Randall, Music by Jerry Moore.

This is the definitive version of the poem,
extensively revised by the author.

BROADSIDE NO. 1, September, 1965
Price: 25 cents
Broadside Press
12651 Old Mill Place
Detroit, Michigan 48238

This version of "Ballad of Birmingham" is the typescript for the broadside and the version recorded by folk singer Jerry Moore in 1965. Despite the declaration that this is the definitive version, Randall alters the last two lines in his 1968 book *Cities Burning.*

Lee and James Boggs." And during "the early 1960s, *Correspondence* published more than half a dozen poems by Dudley Randall . . . [including] 'Ballad of Birmingham,' [which] quickly gained a considerable national notoriety—and wide republication."[3]

This poem transformed Randall's literary life when folk singer Jerry Moore recorded that poem and "Dressed All in Pink," a poem about the assassination of President John F. Kennedy for Blue Note Records in 1965. Prior to the release of the recording, Randall printed the poems as broadsides to protect his rights as the author, and Broadside Press was founded. Randall solicited poems for the *Broadside Series* and titled the first six poems "Poetry of the Negro Revolt." "Ballad of Birmingham" has been reprinted numerous times, and in 2006 it was once again recorded as a song by Santayana Harris.[4] In 1966 Randall expanded his publishing activities at Broadside Press to include poetry books.

In 1969 Randall took a position as a reference librarian at the University of Detroit and was subsequently named poet-in-residence. As his prominence as a poet grew, so did the significance of Broadside Press. Unrestrained by the conventions of mainstream publishing and in tandem with other cultural activities of the Black Arts movement, Randall's efforts effectively broadsided the American literary cannon with a poetry arsenal that was as diverse as its enthusiastic audience. By 1975 the press had published eighty-one books, seventy-four of which were poetry, for an accounting of five hundred thousand books. In addition to bringing the formidable poets Margaret Walker and Sterling Brown back into print, Broadside Press became the publisher for the Pulitzer prize-winning poet Gwendolyn Brooks and for many of the up and coming poets of the Black Arts movement, including Alvin Aubert, James Emanuel, Nikki Giovanni, Etheridge Knight, Don L. Lee (Haki Madhubuti), Audre Lorde, Naomi Madgett, Sonia Sanchez, Alice Walker, and many others. Randall also published the Broadside Critics Series, edited by James Emanuel, and was the distributor for other small presses, including the London-based Breman Press. In addition to his work at Broadside, Randall edited one of the most significant anthologies of African American poetry, *The Black Poets* (Bantam, 1971), which is still in print.

Five of Randall's six poetry books[5] were published during this same period: *Poem Counterpoem* with Margaret Danner (1966), *Cities Burning* (1968), *Love You* (1970), *More to Remember* (1971), and *After the Killing* (1973). His writings appeared in every major anthology of African American literature as well as in

This early handwritten draft of "Dressed All in Pink" was dated "April ? 1964" by Randall.

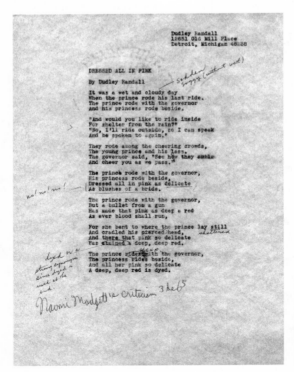

This draft of "Dressed All in Pink" was critiqued by poet Naomi Long Madgett in her handwriting and includes Dudley's verification of her in his handwriting.

DRESSED ALL IN PINK
by Dudley Randall

It was a cloudy, rainy day
When the prince rode his last ride.
The prince rode with the governor
And his princess rode beside.

"And would you like to ride inside
For shelter from the rain?"
"No, I'll ride outside, so I can speak
And be spoken to again."

They rode among the cheering crowds,
The young prince and his lass,
The governor said, "See how they smile
And cheer you as you pass."

The prince rode with the governor,
His princess rode beside,
Dressed all in pink as delicate
As blushes of a bride.

The prince rode with the governor,
But a bullet from a gun
Has stained that pink as deep a red
As ever blood shall run,

For she bent to where the prince lay still
And cradled his pierced head,
And there that pink so delicate
Was stained a deep, deep red.

The prince rode with the governor,
His princess rode beside,
And all her pink so delicate
A deep, deep red was dyed.

——Dudley Randall

Copyright © Dudley Randall 1965
BROADSIDE No. 3
Broadside Press
12651 Old Mill Plac
Detroit Michigan 48238

15 cents

Final draft of "Dressed All in Pink" with edits for a broadside. Randall's handwriting appears in the edits, and he has crossed out Broadside No. 3, perhaps because the poem becomes Broadside No. 2.

numerous collections of American literature. In 1981 after several years of deep emotional depression that nearly resulted in suicide, he published his last collection of poetry, *A Litany of Friends: New and Selected Poems*.

During his lifetime Randall received a number of awards and tributes, some of which include the Wayne State University's Thompkins Award for poetry in 1962 and for fiction in 1964 and a Michigan Council for the Arts Individual Artist Award in 1981. He was twice invited to read his poetry at the Library of Congress, and in 1986 he was the exclusive recipient of the Life Achievement Award from the National Endowment of the Arts. That same year Wayne State University gave him an Honorary Doctor of Letters, and the following year the School of Library Science at the University of Michigan awarded him a Distinguished Alumni Award. He celebrated his eighty-second birthday (January 14, 1996) at the Detroit Institute of Arts for the premiere of the documentary film,

The Black Unicorn: Dudley Randall and the Broadside Press, and during a special celebration in his honor for Black History Month in 1997 the Chrysler Corporation Fund donated an endowed scholarship in his honor to the Department of Africana Studies at Wayne State University. But according to Randall, his most coveted award occurred in 1981 when Mayor Coleman A. Young named him the first poet laureate of the City of Detroit.

Dudley Randall died on August 5, 2000, from congestive heart failure. Subsequently many tributes occurred, the most notable being on May 21, 2001, at the University of Detroit Library, where his place of work was deemed a National Literary Landmark by Friends of the Library of Congress. A bronze plaque with his image was unveiled and appropriately displayed in front of several rows of wooden bookshelves.

These accolades emphasize Dudley Randall's greatness and his courage to elect his own artistic purpose and principles during a cultural revolution to liberate American literature. Appropriately, Randall's poetry has been included in textbooks, translated into several languages, and widely anthologized, including the following mainstream canonical collections: *Modern Poems: An Introduction to Poetry* (Norton, 1976), *The Norton Anthology of Modern Poetry* (Norton, 1988), *The Norton Introduction to Poetry* (Norton, 2006), *The Norton Introduction to Literature* (Norton, 2005), *The Poetry of Black America* (Harper and Row, 1973), *Anthology of Modern American Poetry* (Oxford University Press, 2000), and *Twentieth-Century American Poetry* (McGraw-Hill, 2003). Ironically, none of his poetry was selected for *The Oxford Anthology of African-American Poetry* (Oxford University Press, 2005) or *The Norton Anthology of African American Literature* (Norton, 2003), grave oversights in contemporary African American literary history that *Roses and Revolutions: The Selected Writings of Dudley Randall* aspires to contradict.

The Selected Writings of Dudley Randall

Roses and Revolutions: The Selected Writings of Dudley Randall is arranged in seven sections: "Images from Black Bottom," "Wars: At Home and Abroad," "The Civil Rights Era," "Poems on Miscellaneous Subjects," "Love Poems," "Dialectics of the Black Aesthetic," and "The Last Leap of the Muse." The writings within these thematic topics are organized chronologically. Because many of Randall's poems were composed decades before they were published, this collection is arranged in a more eclectic manner to reflect consistency in intersecting themes as they relate to settings and time frames. Randall's short stories appear in sections related specifically to the historical setting of each story, and because his essays provide context and insight into his poetry, his fiction, and his times, they are situated in sections that correspond with themes and eras that most characterize the creative works. This arrangement facilitates Randall's variegated style within historical context and progression.

The many book reviews that Randall wrote for *Negro Digest* are not included in this collection because they focus on single works and for the most part do not engage broader cultural and social issues. The published interviews of Randall have also been exempted because they are generously integrated into the narrative of the biographical memoir *Wrestling with the Muse,* which also contains composing dates and first publication dates for many poems. This comprehensive study of Randall should be consulted for more extensive literary criticism, for more biographical and historical background on the writer and his times, and for any additional references not provided in the selected bibliography of the present collection. Julius Thompson's *Dudley Randall, Broadside Press, and the Black Arts Movement in Detroit, 1960–1995,* should also be considered for a comprehensive history on Randall's editorial and publishing activities.

The writings presented in this collection represent the latest versions as edited by Dudley Randall. His essay for *A Capsule Course in Black Poetry Writing* (Broadside, 1973) also appears in Appendix II. An extensive bibliography contains many first publications in periodicals as well as primary and secondary references on works by and about Randall. In addition, a DVD of the documentary film *The Black Unicorn: Dudley Randall and the Broadside Press* can be secured through the distributor, Cinema Guild in New York (www.cinemaguild.com).

Composition and Publication Dates

As the executor of Dudley's literary estate, I am responsible for his library, which includes an extensive collection of books and several file cabinets that were obstructed from easy access, and this possibly explained why Dudley had denied that there were any papers or manuscripts available when I was writing his biography. He claimed that he had destroyed all his papers. On the other hand, this misrepresentation assured that I would write a book untainted by interior material, and yet the reason for his glee in response to the completed

Dudley Randall
English 109
1 p.m., M-W-F

OLD WITHERINGTON

Old Witherington had drunk too much again.
The children stopped their play and ganged around him
To jeer his latest brawl; their elders followed.

Prune-black, red-eyed, one-toothed and bullet-headed,
He tottered in the night with legs spread wide.
Waving a hatchet. "Come on, come on!" he shrieked,
"And I'll baptize these bricks with bloody kindling.
I may be old and drunk, but not afraid
To die. I've died before. A million times
I've died and gone to hell. I live in hell.
If I die now I die," And with these words
He damned the giggling children, damned the grinning neighbors,
He damned his father and his mother and his wife,
Himself, and God; all but his adversary, who, crouched,
Danced tenderly round him with a bright-eyed blade.

This early draft of "Old Witherington" was written when Randall was an English major at Wayne State University (1946–51), possibly for a creative writing course, circa 1946–47. It was discovered by the volume editor in 2006.

manuscript was affirmed when I found no inconsistencies between my critical analysis of the poems and what I discovered in his manuscripts, five years after his death and two years after the release of *Wrestling with the Muse*.

Dudley's library was in such disarray that Vivian Randall and I both dreaded the awesome task of sorting through piles of papers, magazines, correspondence, crumpled fliers, faded posters, and Broadside Press administrative documents. As long as Vivian was living, I was able to monitor her husband's literary affairs without any relocation of records or files. But upon Vivian's death on July 28, 2005, Susan West, the attorney for the Randall estate, said that it was necessary to dispose of all material holdings still housed in the Randall home, which was to be sold. The house, which had actually been Vivian's project by design, was a unique quad-level structure with large picture windows and hardwood floors and accented with artwork, oriental rugs, and endless wooden built-in bookcases lining the walls. It was a modest but impressive abode where Dudley's writing and editorial talents blossomed.

In *Wrestling with the Muse*, I propose that many of the love poems were imaginative constructions and should not be mistaken as literal accounts of intimate love affairs. I determined that lines from unfinished love poems written as early as 1943 had been inserted into the 1980 love poems "My Muse" and "To be in Love" and that the poem "Souvenirs," published in 1968, had undergone several transformations since its inception in 1954. The final version evolved into an entirely different form, diverging from its earlier sentimentality and conventional lyrical conformity into a free-verse litany of lines formed by indentations without punctuation. Such evolutionary debarkations echoed Dudley Randall's advice to me in 1972. "Don't discard anything," he said. "You may find use for a line or an image from an earlier, unfinished poem."

What I gleaned from the files were drafts of poems, oftentimes dated to the exact minute. For the purposes of this book, this discovery occurs at the appropriate moment, as specific compositional dates are supplied for most of the writings included in this collection. In particular, the short stories were contained in various drafts, sometimes acquiring new titles as they matured. "A Cup for the Loser" was initially titled "The Race," and "The Cut Throat" was initially titled "The Barber" and was conceived in the third person. "Victoria" was initially titled "Virginia," underwent several drafts until its completion over a period of eight years, and appeared in print in 1962.

In most instances, with the exception of the essays, there is significant disparity between the composition dates and the publication dates, as many of these writings appeared in journals in the 1950s through the 1970s. Some of these dates have been ascertained, but a future exhaustive search to document and detail a complete bibliography of Dudley Randall's work will be pursued in the near future and will accompany the new edition of the biography that will incorporate the findings from his papers. In a few instances no dates were ascertained for some poems. But for the purpose of this collection, the latest confirmed composition date appears at the end of each work, and a complete listing of Randall's poetry books with tables of contents is provided in Appendix I.

Essays as Context

For the most part, Randall's essays are about poets and poetry and thereby reveal his perspective on poetics and aesthetics. His essays rarely address subjects outside of literature, but in those few instances where he inserts his political views, he is very specific about his aversion to dogma and ideologues. This perspective is the result of his extensive knowledge of world history and how censorship represses creative instincts and expression. He regarded racial discrimination in publishing as a form of censorship; hence, his views as an editor, critic, publisher, and poet were aligned with aesthetic freedom. At the same time, he engaged the subjects of race and writing from this perspective: "How else can a black writer write than out of his black experience? Yet, what we tend to overlook is that our common humanity makes it possible to write a love poem, for instance, without a word of race, or to write a nationalistic poem that will be valid for all humanity, such as 'By the waters of Babylon, there we sat down, yea, we wept when we remembered Zion.'"[6]

"The Black Aesthetic in the Thirties, Forties, and Fifties"[7] is a critical link to understanding Randall's literary origin and aesthetic politics. This essay discusses the historical forces and poetic practices that influenced emerging African American poets of his generation. He analyzes the writings of those poets he regards as the most prominent in terms of publications and literary influence: Robert Hayden, Margaret Walker, Melvin B. Tolson, Sterling Brown, Gwendolyn Brooks, and Frank Marshall Davis. Randall does not reference himself in this essay, but he does group his poetry with theirs in the section "Post-Renaissance" in his seminal anthology, *The Black Poets*. With regard to Randall's literary techniques, this essay on the Post-Harlem Renaissance era is especially insightful because these writers are his contemporaries, and his work reflects similar poetic strategies.

Randall provides a framework for this historical period through aesthetic comparisons with the Harlem Renaissance that preceded it and the Black Arts movement that followed this intermediary period. In order to introduce the dialectic of racial identity and individuality in the consciousness of the black aesthetic, Randall quotes the 1926 essay "The Negro Artist and the Racial Mountain"[8] by Langston Hughes (whose poetry spans all three periods). Randall explains that "Hughes makes a distinction between racial pride and aesthetic freedom for the individual writer," and Randall contrasts Hughes's perspective with the dominant view of the Black Arts era: "In the Black Aesthetic, individualism is frowned upon. Feedback from black people, or the mandates of self-appointed literary commissars, is supposed to guide the poet." More emphatically, Randall states, "In my own opinion, this feedback usually comes from the most vocal group, ideologues or politicians, who are eager to use the persuasiveness of literature to seize or consolidate power for themselves. Politicians such as Stalin or Khrushchev have a certain low cunning, but they cannot grasp the complexity or paradoxes of life and literature, and they try to impose their own simple-mindedness and conformity upon them."

Randall's allusion to Stalin and Khrushchev, two repressive Soviet dictators, is a metaphorical critique of political dogma interfering with the aesthetic expressions of black writers during the Black Arts movement. As a labor rights advocate, socialist sympathizer, and scholar of Russian poetry before and after the Great Revolution, Randall's critique is not a snide comment. This opinion resurfaces as outright defiance in response to aesthetic repression in his 1981 poem "A Poet Is Not a Jukebox" after some black writers criticized his interest in bawdy poetry and derided him for not writing about current social and political issues:

Telling a Black poet what he ought to write
Is like some Commissar of Culture in Russia telling a poet
He'd better write about the new steel furnaces in the Novobigorsk
   region,
Or the heroic feats of Soviet labor in digging the trans-Caucausus
   Canal,
Or the unprecedented achievement of workers in the sugar beet indus-
   try who exceeded their quota by 400 per cent (it was later discovered
   to be a typist's error).

As the poem continues, Randall asserts:

> I'll bet you in a hundred years the poems the Russian people will read,
>   sing, and love
> Will be poems about his mother's death, his unfaithful mistress, or his
>   wine, roses and nightingales,
> Not the poems about steel furnaces, the trans-Caucausus Canal, or the
>   sugar beet industry.
> A poet writes about what he feels, what agitates his heart and sets his
>   pen in motion.
> Not what some apparatchnik dictates, to promote his own career or
>   theories.
> Yeah, maybe I'll write about Miami, as I wrote about Birmingham.[9]
> But it'll be because I want to write about Miami,[10] not because some-
>   body says I ought to.

Conversely, the working class consciousness that surfaces in Randall's poetry was nurtured during his involvement with the labor movement and his interactions with American socialists and communists. Randall's "George" (ca. 1960) celebrates a foundry worker he once knew in the 1930s:

> When I was a boy desiring the title of man
> And toiling to earn it
> In the inferno of the foundry knockout,
> I watched and admired you working by my side,
> As, goggled, with mask on your mouth and shoulders bright with
>   sweat,
> You mastered the monstrous, lumpish cylinder blocks,
> And when they clotted the line and plunged to the floor,
> With force enough to tear your foot in two,
> You calmly stepped aside.

Likewise, his poem "Ancestors" interjects class consciousness at the height of racial essentialism during the Black Power movement:

> Why are our ancestors
> always kings or princes
> and never the common people?

Was the Old Country a democracy
where every man was a king?
Or did all the slavecatchers
steal only the aristocrats
and leave the fieldhands
laborers
streetcleaners
garbage collectors
dishwashers
cooks
and maids
behind?

Although these poems were composed during the 1960s and 1970s, they are grounded and reference to Randall's labor activism during the 1930s and 1940s and thereby demonstrate a continuum in his class consciousness. Both Hayden and Randall grew up in Detroit's Black Bottom, and much of their imagery and many of their personae emerge from this neighborhood, where class and race converged. Among Randall's earlier poems, "Old Witherington" and "For Pharish Pinckney, Bindle-Stiff during the Depression" emphasize a strong appreciation for working-class culture and community.

Thematic focus on the common folk recurs in many of his poems in tandem with the perspective of most post-Renaissance poets. Randall explains this as an extension of Harlem Renaissance poetry, but by contrast "the new patterns in imagery are not picaresque and break with traditional poetic forms."[11] This essay gives insight into how Randall negotiated literary techniques, rejected the obscurity of many Modernist poets, and merged folk and literary forms to the advantage of his cultural diversity as a black writer. He mastered conventional forms and African American poetics, which were adapted from music and folk expressions. "The Southern Road," an often anthologized poem and an allusion to a book of poetry by Sterling Brown, reflects Randall's capacity to merge a traditional ballad with other structural techniques and reiterates his stylistic interest in contradiction and ambiguity. The poem contrasts the presence of churches on the landscape with the horrors of lynching and burnings of black victims. The atrocities are conveyed through images of human fragments, as mutilated and charred bodies evince and answer the poet's internal voice:[12]

And I re-live the enforced avatar
Of shuddering journey to a strange abode
Made by my sires before another war;
And I set forth upon the southern road.
. . . .
O fertile hillsides where my fathers are,
And whence my griefs like troubled streams have flowed,
Love you I must, though they may sweep me far,
And I set forth upon the southern road.

I conceived "The Southern Road" while traveling to basic training center in the South in 1943, but I didn't write the poem until after the war, in 1948. I enjoyed writing "The Southern Road" because of problems of craftsmanship. I admired the poems of Francois Villon. Villon was a fourteenth-century Frenchman who was a vagabond, a thief, and a murderer. But his "Ballade of the Dead Queens," his "Ballade of His Mother to the Virgin Mary," and his "Ballade Written the Night Before He Was To Be Hanged" are some of the most powerful poems ever written.[13]

In the African American literary tradition, Randall frequently engaged historical subjects. "Booker T. and W. E. B." (1952) is one of his more famous pieces. Published at the dawn of the modern civil rights movement, this poem encapsulates an irreconcilable argument between two legendary political leaders in language that communicates to audiences of all ages and educational levels. In a terse debate intensified by the restraint of rhyme, Randall captures the essence of the ideological differences between Booker T. Washington and W. E. B. Du Bois:

"It seems to me," said Booker T.,
"It shows a mighty lot of cheek
To study chemistry and Greek
When Mister Charlie needs a hand
To hoe the cotton on his land,
And when Miss Anne looks for a cook,
Why stick your nose inside a book?"

"I don't agree," said W. E. B.
"If I should have the drive to seek
Knowledge of chemistry or Greek,
I'll do it. Charles and Miss can look
Another place for hand or cook.
Some men rejoice in skill of hand,
And some in cultivating land,
But there are others who maintain
The right to cultivate the brain."

This poem is one of Randall's most anthologized and quoted because the argument continues to be debated by scholars and laypersons. A decade later the poem was interpreted into a visual work of art by Shirley Woodson Reid and contains handwritten lines by Randall. (A print of that artistic collaboration appears on the cover of this book.)

In literary history, another disagreement is presented in Randall's essay "White Poet, Black Critic,"[14] which frames the civil rights era as it reveals the conscious and unconscious racism of Robert Frost, the famous American poet, and the failed attempts of Stanley Braithwaite, the black poet and critic, to transcend a racialized literary society. Although this terse and pointed essay illustrates the practice of racial prejudice in literary society, the purpose is not simply to expose Frost or to advise Braithwaite but rather to encourage writers to be mindful of the politics of race and to not deny their identity in pursuit of publication, a point that is echoed in a later essay in *A Capsule Course in Black Poetry Writing*. A similar experience is discussed by Randall in "Melvin B. Tolson: Portrait of a Poet as Raconteur,"[15] when Tolson appealed to Allen Tate to write an introduction for his famous long poem "Libretto for the Republic of Liberia," and Tate "replied that he wasn't interested in the propaganda of Negro poets." In three of his essays Randall focuses on Melvin B. Tolson, deliberations that should receive renewed interest because of Denzel Washington's recent portrayal of Tolson as a professor and debate coach at Wiley College in the popular film *The Great Debaters* (released December 2007).

Within a broader context, the theme of cultural identity is pursued in "Toward Mount Olympus: Ubi Sunt and Hic Sum."[16] In this essay Randall explains the subconscious elicitations of recurrent poetic structures on the part of poets because of historical circumstances and a need to affirm identity.[17] "Ubi sunt" appears in Melvin B. Tolson's "Harlem Gallery," and "Hic sum" or "Here

I am" is an extension of this strategy in Langston Hughes's "A Negro Speaks of Rivers." Through his knowledge of Villon, Randall cleverly demonstrates the universality of certain themes and connects them to black poets who have been dismissed by critics for using poetry in the service of so-called Negro propaganda. His conclusion affirms such thematic inspirations as in Walt Whitman's transcendence of "Ubi sunt" or "Hic sum" as he claims the magnificence of the present as himself in "Leaves of Grass." Indeed, this level of cultural confidence is reflected in Randall's "Roses and Revolutions."

Dialectics of the Black Arts Movement

"Black Power" is a piece Randall wrote in response to an invitation from Hoyt Fuller to be included in a special issue of *Negro Digest* on the subject. This essay, more than any other piece, presents Randall's political views in plain language. He argues in favor of Black Power but in his usual manner defines the term on his own terms: "In my opinion, Black Power means organizing black people so that they can have power commensurate with their numbers in their communities, states, and in the nation. This will mean that they may dominate some communities politically, will be a strong force in some states, and will wield power in the national government. This is similar to what other groups have done."[18]

Randall's view is as balanced as his editorial policies at Broadside Press and the political dialectics in his poetry. He advocates for varied voices to be heard in political discussions in order to deal with the vicissitudes of racial injustice. He opens by criticizing the excessive arguments between civil rights organizations and the destructive and adverse consequences of such infighting. He agrees with many sides of the argument but within context and with relativity. However, his particular concern is the larger prose of racial progress intoned with the need for self-defense. As a language person, he focuses on the impact that the term has had on society and a typical white response to Black Power because of historical mistreatment of blacks: "When you have kidnapped, enslaved, beaten, murdered, raped, exploited, cheated, traduced, and committed injustice toward a race for over 300 years, how can you escape feelings of guilt, and the fear that they will do to you what you have done to them?"

In this short but intense essay, the various angles of Randall's discourse intersect with a number of his poems, especially "Black Poet, White Critic" and "The Melting Pot," as well as his satirical pieces "The Intellectuals," "Seeds of

Revolution," "Put Your Muzzle Where Your Mouth Is (Or Shut Up)," and "Abu." In these poems he counters reactionary activists by presenting absurd contradictions and even dangerous consequences in their careless rhetoric and mindless politics. By contrast, his graphic poem "Sniper" projects a poignant understanding of self-defense as revolutionary action during the 1967 Detroit Rebellion (Race Riot):

Somewhere
On a rooftop
You fight for me.

"Black Publisher, Black Writer: An Answer,"[19] which also appears in the section "Dialectics of the Black Aesthetic," is Randall's response to an essay by novelist and poet John A. Williams wherein Williams expresses his disenchantment with black publishers. The rhetorical structure of the title of Randall's essay parallels his essay "White Writer, Black Critic" and his poem "Black Poet, White Critic." In "Black Publisher, Black Writer: An Answer" he introduces the economic factors that limit the productivity and the choices of black publishers, and at the end of the essay he contrasts the amazing accomplishments of black authors with these institutions and envisions unlimited possibilities through the efforts of innovative editors.

As a student of foreign languages and world literatures, Randall optimized and complicated his vocabulary. The creative value of this extensive reservoir is detailed in an essay for the handbook *A Capsule Course in Black Poetry Writing*.[20] His humorous opening entices the reader to engage a topic he is fiercely serious about—poetry—and the discussion that ensues challenges aspiring poets to consider a regimen that probably won't result in fame, wealth, or political prominence, which he insists is not the purpose of poetry. In this essay Randall discusses skill, knowledge, poetics, history, culture, and thematic purpose. He consistently urges writers to develop their craft by knowing all facets of the genre. This essay is an excellent minicourse in creative writing and includes discussions on poetics, diction, publishing protocol, and commitment to style and recommendations on how to become knowledgeable without diminishing one's identity while creating work that is larger than anyone's particular experience. In addition to the purpose for which it was written, this essay provides access to the complex dimensions of Randall's poetry, is a guide to his approaches and techniques in his earlier poems, and provides perspective for his later works. Because of the technicality and the length of this essay, it is included as Appendix II.

"Black Emotion and Experience: The Literature for Understanding" is a bibliographical essay that was published in *American Libraries*.[21] Randall attempts to explain emotion as an aesthetic characteristic of African American literature in general and in Black Arts poetry in particular. The essay appears at the end of the section "Dialectics of the Black Aesthetic" because it is the appropriate position for this comprehensive overview of the era. He opens the essay with an emotional experience that he translated into the poem "Slave Castle": "I took movies of black American students coming out of the dungeons of the former slaved castle in Elmina, Ghana. The tour of the castle was a profoundly moving experience for us. Probably all of us thought, 'Long ago our mothers and fathers passed through just such a place as this. People like us suffered and died here.' Our emotional upheaval was evident in facial expression, gestures   words   tears."[22]

Randall's poems "Ancestors," "A Different Image," and "African Suite" demonstrate the perspective of an empathetic descendant respectful of his African heritage and critical of contemporary neocolonial exploitation of the continent but mindful of his American historical reality and identity. And, he connects the origin of African Americans at the point of divergence in Black American literature relative to American literature: "This qualitative difference of emotion and experience is what strikes one in black American literature. Not only was there a difference in the way blacks came here; there is also a difference in the way blacks regard American myths and heroes. Whites revere George Washington of the cherry tree incident. Black poet June Jordan says, 'George Washington he think he big / He trade my father for a pig.'"

Randall provides an overview of African American literature by illustrating the trends and developments in the black aesthetic and white literary establishment's resistance to perspectives and themes that distinguish the African American historical experience. It is an excellent guide and introduction to the literature and demonstrates the connection between Randall's special literary interests, his knowledge as teacher, and his bibliographical contribution as a librarian. This work as well as his other essays evince a broad and deep knowledge of literature and languages and his capacity to make aesthetic connections across continents and centuries. His short stories, however, display this same precision and depth of intellect in African American cultural experiences.

Short Fiction

Dudley Randall wrote only five works of fiction. "A Cup for the Loser" was published in *The Negro History Bulletin*,[23] and "Victoria," "Incident on a Bus," "The Cut Throat," and "Shoe Shine Boy" were published in Hoyt Fuller's *Negro Digest*.[24] In this collection, the stories are arranged according to their historical settings: "Incident on a Bus" and "Shoe Shine Boy" reflect the civil rights era; "The Cut Throat," "A Cup for the Loser," and "Victoria" reminisce the fertile grounds of Black Bottom circa the 1930s. The two latter stories are told from the perspective of the character David, who has some autobiographical features of Randall. David is also the narrator and silent observer in "A Cup for the Loser" who tells a story about his father and a roomer in their home. In "Victoria" the story emanates from David's perspective as well, but in this story the theme revolves around his infatuation with a teenage girl. These two stories embellish set description and contain more action and are considerably longer than the other three.

In "A Cup for the Loser" Randall seems to have fashioned David's father after his own. Arthur Randall loved to debate, which was a major distinction between father and son, and this story supports Randall's view that arguing with others is pointless. Papa (David's father) and Arthur Randall both worked in the automobile foundry, and as in the story Arthur Randall also took in boarders to help pay the mortgage during the Great Depression. Other parallels are that Papa is athletic and is an avid reader. As a minister, Arthur Randall was also a temperance advocate, and this story, which takes place during Prohibition, is about an argument between David's father and Mr. Goodlow about the "evils of drinking." Despite Randall's inadvertent criticism of his father, Papa is credited for his informed logic and steadfast integrity in this nuanced characterization.

In a letter to Robert Hayden (August 29, 1966), Randall wrote: "Did you read my story in the May Digest? Will take you back to Black Bottom, in spite of the false illustration."[25] Randall reached back to his teen years to create the characters and the setting for the short story "Victoria." David, the main character, desires Victoria, who is an orphan, as in the case of Randall's first wife Ruby. Like Randall, David is a bookworm and an athlete who studies Italian because he admires Dante and wishes to write a great love poem for Victoria. As Randall explains in *Wrestling with the Muse*, his earliest motivation to write poetry was "to impress a girl with hazel eyes" when he was a teenager.[26] David's attraction to Victoria includes her physical beauty, her independent spirit, her intelligence, and her athleticism. Randall's full appreciation of the feminine gender advocates a progressive view that anticipates male enlightenment after the women's movement of the 1970s. Even David's sister, Rachel, resembles Randall's sister, Esther, who is outgoing and encourages David to go after Victoria instead of pining in the background. The setting of the gym where young men aspire to be boxers typifies the era and connects with the neighborhood and Detroit's famous fighter, Joe Louis. It is the longest of Randall's short stories and in many ways reflects his shy personality and interior imagination:

> David's glance wandered over the field flooded with sunshine. A group of boys and a group of girls were playing baseball, and smaller children were climbing on the swing supports and horizontal bars. Near the alley, some older youths were playing dice, with one on the lookout for the roaches. The bright shirts and dresses, the movements of the ball players, the crack of the bats on balls and the shouts of the players made the field a world of color and motion and sound.
>
> David projected himself into the scene. He was striking the ball, running the bases. He was crouched in the corner over the dice, caressing them and talking to them like a lover. While he was immersed in these actions he was aware of another self that stood aloof and watched him doing these things, and of yet another self that watched him watching himself, like a series of mirrors.

Love is the dominant theme in Randall's poetry, and it is the theme that sustains his longest short story and the strongest inspiration for his writing. But political themes occur in "Incident on a Bus" and "Shoe Shine Boy."

"Incident on a Bus" takes place in the South after a bus boycott organized by a civil rights organization. In this short, short story with a constrained setting, Randall's verbal economy manages to contextualize the historical dynamics of peaceful protest threatened by violent attacks by the Ku Klux Klan. By inverting the assumed behavior of a "nondescript Negro" and exposing his invisibility in society, Randall forewarns the audience of the possibility of a violent response if peaceful strategies are not effective. It also foreshadows the Black Power movement and many of his poems collected in *After the Killing*.

The 1960s in the men's room is the setting for "Shoe Shine Boy." The simplicity of the setting provides a context for conflicting notions about masculinity and contrasting forms of war as two very distinct characters, a white army sergeant and a black civil rights worker, interact with Alexander the shoe shine boy, an elderly gentleman and the focal point of the story. He appears to be a stereotypical Negro who grins, bugs his eyes, and tap dances to entertain whites in order to secure tips. The offensive voice of the sergeant reemerges in the poem "Straight Talk from a Patriot." Accordingly, the civil rights activist abhors this behavior; however, a twist at the end of the story reveals another dimension to Alexander. This theme is also pursued in Randall's poem "Seeds of Revolution":

> The Revolution
> did not begin in 1966
> when Stokely raised his fist
> and shouted, Black power.
>
> Nor did it begin last year
> when you read Fanon
> and discovered you were black.

Just as in "Shoe Shine Boy," the interior stanzas of the poem propose different acts of rebellion and resistance, such as a black on a slave ship leaping overboard or as an Uncle Tom outsmarting the white supremacist arrogance of the slave master.

The structure of the short story "The Cut Throat" is even more contained and apolitical. There are no temporal or cultural references in the story, so the racial identity of the main character is inconsequential, while this introspective characterization suggests some psychological aspects of the author. The story takes place in a barbershop and in the imagination of a barber, who tells a bizarre story about an attempted murder. The word "cut" in the title acts as both a verb and an adjective, and this ambiguity undergirds dramatic tension and an unanticipated ending in this adaptation of the styles of Edgar Allen Poe and O. Henry. Despite the favorable reception of his short fiction, including the Thompkins Award in 1964, Randall shortly thereafter abandoned the short story and focused his creative writing exclusively on poetry.

The Heart of the Writings: The Poetry

Poet and publisher Naomi Madgett explains in *The Oxford Companion to African American Literature*:

A distinctive style is difficult to identify in Randall's poetry. In his early poems he was primarily concerned with construction. Many of those in *More to Remember* are written in such fixed forms as the haiku, triolet, dramatic monologue, and sonnet while others experiment with slant rhyme, indentation, and the blues form. He later concentrated on imagery and phrasing, yet some of his more recent work continues to suggest the styles of other poets. Although many of these move with more freedom, originality, and depth of feeling, and encompass a wider range of themes, others identifiable by printed date demonstrate a return to traditional form.[27]

Randall's variegated style emanated from his mastery of conventional forms and his adaptation of African American cultural expressions. For example, he used the blues to grieve the death of Langston Hughes in "Langston Blues" and the gospel to mourn the assassination of Malcolm X, Medgar Evers, and Martin Luther King Jr. in "Blood Precious Blood." On the other hand, Randall's preference for sonnets includes a study of its origin in thirteenth-century Sicilian love poetry. Randall's "April Mood" is a Spenserian sonnet, which resembles the Italian sonnet with a difficult, interlinking rhyme scheme. Similar to Gwendolyn Brooks, he often employed the sonnet, especially in the construction of love poems, and his variations in sonnets was extensive, including those found in English and Italian literatures.

The sonnet "Anniversary Words," dedicated to his wife Vivian, combines a rush of images that run together like the habitual years of marriage, emphasizing Randall's disruptive messiness and Vivian's irritated tolerance as the couple reconciles conflicting habits and minor maladjustments. The poem illustrates the intimacy of nonverbal exchange between partners and the emotional convergence that binds and centers them:[28]

> despite the absent-mindedness of my ways
> and the not seldom acerbity of your tone,
> I sometimes catch a softness in your gaze
> which tells me after all I am your own
> and that you love me in no little way.
> But I know it best by the things you never say.

Likewise, Randall's translations of Russian poetry are love poems. He studied the poetry of Konstantin Simonov, who was well known for his wartime love poetry and his novel *Days and Nights* about the Soviet Union's resistance to Nazi aggression. Randall's thematic interests converge with writers who wrote against fascism and pursued romantic lyricism. He explained that the poetry of Simonov was very popular during World War II because

> Russian soldiers would send copies of the poems to their girl friends or wives. There are different theories about translation. My own is that I try to translate in the meter of the original. I believe that the music of the poem is very important, and I try to recapture some of that music in English, or to find an English equivalent:[29]

> Son and mother may believe
> That I am no more,
> Friends may give me up and grieve,
> And may sit before
> The fire, drinking bitter wine
> To my memory.
> Wait. And with them gathered there
> Do not drink to me.

Randall commands an assertive and yet somber tone in "I Loved You Once," a translation of Alexander Pushkin's "Ya Vas Lyubil." The depth and desperate passion in Pushkin's poem reemerge in the same number of lines and similar syllabic configurations for a facsimile of the original. Just as Randall often referenced Terence, the Roman African writer,[30] his study of Pushkin, the black Russian poet, demonstrates his internationalism and his racial awareness, an alternative universalism that transcends the conventional perception of the term that ignores racial diversity in Western civilization.

This intercontinental consciousness is likewise illustrated in Randall's poems about Africa, as his poetry forms a continuum from the past to present African American sensibilities. These poems supersede rhetorical didacticism that obstructed many Black Arts poems on similar subjects. For example, in "Slave Castle (Elmina, Ghana)" he portrays a poignant encounter with a relic of the slave trade by infusing the solemnity of the experience with the slave spiritual, "Crucifixion." As in "Blood Precious Blood," Randall associates memory and emotional intensity by adapting a song derived from suffering through slavery: "Many people who were not well educated and who knew few books beyond the Bible, yet were able to speak and write with eloquence because they had absorbed some of the beauty of that book. Think of the songs of the slave singers."[31]

In another thematic shift, the publication of *Love You* (1970) during the Black Arts movement articulated a softer mood in a literary atmosphere fueled with aesthetic anger. Despite the urgency of cultural conflict and political confrontation, Randall's dedication to love poetry illuminated an oppositional current in his aesthetic expressions. To reiterate this point, he submitted four love poems to the September 1970 poetry issue of *Black World* (formerly *Negro Digest*), an obvious statement about aesthetic freedom considering the militant themes that dominated this issue. About the political dialectic in one of his love poems, Randall stated: "'The Profile on the Pillow' was written in the late 1960s, in a time when cities were burning and there were rumors that the government was preparing concentration camps for black Americans, like the camps for Japanese-Americans in World War II. I tried to make it powerful by enclosing conflicting emotions in the same poem—love and fear, tenderness and terror. The tension of the times made writing that poem a powerful experience."[32]

Randall also engaged the cultural wars that beset the Black Arts movement with poems that were designed to transform incite into insight. One of the best examples of this is "An Answer to Lerone Bennett's Questionnaire On a Name for Black Americans" (1968), which unravels the debate that divided black writers at the 1966 Fisk Writers Conference and throughout subsequent decades:

Discarding the Spanish word for black
and taking the Anglo-Saxon word for Negro,
discarding the names of English slavemasters
and taking the names of Arabian slave-traders
won't put a single
bean in your belly
or an inch of steel
in your spine.

In this poem, the syndrome of name changes for "the race" is related to an identity crisis in the intellectual community. The chronicling of various imperialist slave traders illustrates the futility of attempted escape from history and an unnecessary obsession with it. Randall contracts the abstract absurdity of such rationalization with material reality:

> won't put a single
> bean in your belly
> or an inch of steel
> in your spine.

This leveling is accentuated by humorously inverting imagery from Shakespeare, "a rose by any other name is just as sweet," into "Call a skunk a rose, / and he'll still stink," and then reversing it with: "Call a rose a skunk, / and it'll still smell sweet." Even more emphatically, it will "even sweeten the name." As in "Put Your Muzzle Where Your Mouth Is," "The Idiot," "Informer," "F.B.I. Memo," and "Abu," Randall uses humor to soften the aggressive tone in these poems that identify political and ideological contradictions. "A Leader of the People" engages a similar theme, but the mood in this poem is more pensive.

At the same time, Randall was influenced by the new poetics of the Black Arts movement and by the more inclusive audiences:

> In my own poetry, I no longer strive for the intricate, sonorous stanzas of "The Southern Road." I try for a looser form, a more colloquial diction, as in "Frederick Douglass and the Slave Breaker."[33] I want my poems to be read and understood by children, students, farmers, factory workers, professors. I seek directness and lucidity, but a richness so that the reader will find added meanings on each new reading. I avoid eccentricities and grotesqueries.
>
> I enjoyed writing "Frederick Douglass and the Slave Breaker" because it was a commissioned poem and because it took its place in the poetic tradition. I was asked to write a poem for the dedication of the murals in the Frederick Douglass Branch Library in Detroit. I knew that two other poets, Robert Hayden and Langston Hughes, had already written two famous poems about Douglass, so I was treading on hallowed ground. One day I was in the studio of the painter, Leroy Foster, and saw his painting for the mural. It was not the familiar Frederick Douglass, with a long beard. It was a bare torso of a beardless boy. At once I said, "That's the teenage Douglass when he fought old Cosey, the black slave-breaker." I knew I had found my subject. It was enjoyable to join the company of two fine poets like Hughes and Hayden.[34]

In many ways, Randall executed his own poetry revolution. He angled his poetry to counter and to complement popular trends in Black American and American poetry. Most poetry written during the Black Arts movement was free verse, which related to the attitude of era, as was also the case with Randall. The poem "The Dilemma" delineates a disagreement with critics who celebrate obscurity in poetry and a perspective Randall expresses as a stylistic shift in his later poems. Consistently, however, his election of forms was dictated by themes. In a review of Randall's *After the Killing* (1973) that appeared in the *American Poetry Review*, poet June Jordan acknowledges Randall's clever contrariness: "In the most delightful, benevolent sense of the word, he chooses, rather, to teach, and he chooses not to exclude himself from the teaching, as in 'Tell It Like It Is.'" Jordan also recognizes Randall's aesthetic diversity: "Brother Randall opts for comparatively formalist constructions of his poems; they hit/ they land like glowing stones." About his style, she says that his writing is sometimes "lucid and succinct," "wry and sly," and "elsewhere, in the folio you will find the poems, by turns, working within the blues idiom, or falling out, limpid and gentle, in a convincing, lyric line. There is much direct warmth, and felt, epigrammatic economy, among these distinctive poems."[35]

Even when Randall's words countered the obscured vision of the younger generation, he was still supportive of their writing careers and consistently critical of an insensitive status quo. In agreement with the quest for new poetics, he broke with conventions and challenged cultural imperialism, as articulated in "Black Poet, White Critic." His ultimate goal during the Black Arts era was to push rhetoric to substance and to transform language into action.

Despite societal prejudice, political disruptions, or personal devastation, throughout Dudley Randall's literary career his pen divulged societal inequities while contouring the nuances of humanity's contradictions. Ironically, or appropriately, the most luminary poems in his last poetry collection exhibit a stylistic return to somber imagery and subtle sonic patterns that were honed during his most prolific period, the early 1960s, before Broadside Press dominated his literary activities. The chiseled imagery and finely tuned rhythmic measures in "To an Old Man" and "Bag Woman" reclaim the mastery of "George" and "Frederick Douglass and the Slave Breaker." In his essay "Endowing the World and Time: The Life and Work of Dudley Randall," R. Baxter Miller states that Randall's last book of poems, *A Litany of Friends: New and Selected Poems* (1981), "demonstrates an intellectual depth of themes and technical mastery of the poetic form."[36]

Roses and Revolutions complements Randall's thematic and artistic repertoire in *A Litany of Friends* by presenting his most exemplary poetry. The book also extends his literary largesse by collecting his short stories, which are rare gems retrieved from classic periodicals, and his essays, which profoundly affected philosophical discourse on the Black Aesthetic during the 1960s and 1970s. Ultimately, and hopefully, *Roses and Revolutions: The Selected Writings of Dudley Randall* best demonstrates Randall's skills as a wordsmith, his influence as a literary forerunner, and his revolutionary spirit that no one, black or white, could tell what to write.

Notes

1. Dudley Randall, as quoted in A. X. Nicholas, "A Conversation with Dudley Randall," *Black World* 21, no. 11 (December 1971): 33.

2. The Correspondence Publishing Committee was initially founded by C. L. R. James and Roya Dunayeuskaya. After the forced deportation of James to Great Britain in 1953 and various ideological and political splits in the organization, the Bogges became the editors of the publication in the 1960s.

3. James Edward Smethhurst, *The Black Arts Movement: Literary Nationalism in the 1960s and 1970s* (Chapel Hill and London: University of North Carolina Press, 2005), 191.

4. Santayana Harris was a music student at Tennessee State University at the time of the recording.

5. Poetry books by Dudley Randall: *Poem Counterpoem* with Margaret Danner (Detroit: Broadside, 1966), *Cities Burning* (Detroit: Broadside, 1968), *Love You* (London: Bremen, 1970), *More to Remember* (Chicago: Third World, 1971), *After the Killing* (Chicago: Third World, 1973), and *A Litany of Friends: New and Selected Poems* (Detroit: Lotus, 1981).

6. Dudley Randall interview in "Black Writer's Views on Literary Lions and Values," *Negro Digest* 17, no. 3 (January 1968): 42.

7. Dudley Randall, "The Black Aesthetic in the Thirties, Forties, and Fifties," in *The Black Aesthetic,* edited by Addison Gayle Jr., 235–45 (Garden City, NY: Doubleday, 1971).

8. "The Negro Artist and the Racial Mountain" by Langston Hughes was initially published in 1926 in *The Nation* and was reprinted in *The Black Aesthetic.*

9. "Ballad of Birmingham" (1963), one of Randall's more famous poems, is alluded to in "A Poet Is Not a Jukebox" to demonstrate his political aesthetic.

10. Randall, "The Black Aesthetic in the Thirties, Forties, and Fifties," 240–41.

11. This is a reference to the race riot in Miami, Florida, in 1980.

12. "The Southern Road," "grim through classical allusions to Hades, and mixing love, hatred, beauty, and bestiality, is Randall's best expression of ancestral and racial devotion, conveyed almost hypnotically in the refrain." James A. Emanuel and Theodore L. Gross, eds., *Dark Symphony: Negro Literature in America* (New York: Free Press, 1968), 489.

13. Dudley Randall, quoted in D. H. Melhem, *Heroism in Black Poetry* (Lexington: University Press of Kentucky, 1990), 58–60.

14. Dudley Randall, "White Poet, Black Critic," *Negro Digest* 14, no. 4 (February 1965): 46–48.

15. Dudley Randall, "Melvin B. Tolson: Portrait of a Poet Raconteur," *Negro Digest* 15, no. 3 (January 1966): 54–57.

16. Dudley Randall, "Toward Mount Olympus: Ubi Sunt and Hic Sum," *Negro Digest* 14, no. 11 (September 1965): 73–76.

17. "Ubi sunt" (Latin for "Where are they?") was a poetic innovation of the fourteenth-century French poet Francois Villon that influenced poets for centuries.

18. Dudley Randall, "Black Power," *Negro Digest* 16, no. 1 (November 1966): 95–96.

19. Dudley Randall, "Black Publisher, Black Writer: An Answer," *Black World* 24, no. 5 (March 1975): 30–37.

20. Dudley Randall, *A Capsule Course in Black Poetry Writing* (Detroit: Broadside, 1975).

21. Dudley Randall, "Black Emotion and Experience: The Literature for Understanding," *American Libraries* 4 (February 1973): 86–90.

22. Ibid, 88.

23. Dudley Randall, "A Cup for the Loser," *Negro History Bulletin* 26, no. 1 (October 1962): 85.

24. Dudley Randall, "Incident on a Bus," *Negro Digest* 14, no. 10 (August 1965): 70–71; "Victoria," *Negro Digest* 15, no. 7 (May 1966); "The Cut Throat," *Negro Digest* 13, no. 9 (July 1964): 53–56; "Shoe Shine Boy," *Negro Digest* 15, no. 11 (September 1966): 53–55.

25. Dudley Randall to Robert Hayden, August 29, 1966, Robert Hayden Papers, National Baha'i Archives, Box 5, Wilmette, Illinois.

26. Melba Joyce Boyd, *Wrestling with the Muse: Dudley Randall and the Broadside Press* (New York: Columbia University Press, 2003), 44.

27. Naomi Madgett, "Dudley Randall," in *Oxford Companion to African American Literature* (New York: Oxford University Press, 1997), 620–21.

28. Randall craftily improvises on the Spenserian sonnet: ababba abbba eded ee, with the structural distinction of the Elizabethan sonnet, which comprise two stanzas, an octave and a sextet. Randall further improvises the form by ending all but two of the lines with a comma, thereby running the sound pattern and the imagery of the octave into the sextet.

29. Dudley Randall, "A Conversation with Dudley Randall," by A. X. Nicholas, *Black World* 21, no. 11 (December 1971): 29.

30. Dudley Randall, as quoted in "A Conversation with Dudley Randall," by A. X. Nicholas, *Black World* 21, no. 11 (December 1971): 33; and Dudley Randall, ed., *A Capsule Course in Black Poetry Writing* (Detroit: Broadside, 1975).

31. Randall, "A Capsule Course in Black Poetry Writing."

32. Gwendolyn Fowlkes, "An Interview with Dudley Randall," *Black Scholar* 6, no. 6 (June 1975): 89.

33. "Frederick Douglass and the Slave Breaker" was derived from a painting by Leroy Foster and a story from Douglass's autobiography, *The Life and Times of Frederick Douglass* (1881).

34. Fowlkes, "An Interview with Dudley Randall," 89.

35. June Jordan, Review of *After the Killing, American Poetry Review* 3, no. 2 (March/April 1974): 32.

36. R. Baxter Miller, "Endowing the World and Time: The Life and Work of Dudley Randall," in *Black American Poets between Worlds, 1940-1960,* edited by R. Baxter Miller, 77–92 (Knoxville: University of Tennessee Press, 1966), 89.

Roses and Revolutions

Musing on roses and revolutions,
I saw night close down on the earth like a great dark wing,
and the lighted cities were like tapers in the night,
and I heard the lamentations of a million hearts
regretting life and crying for the grave,
and I saw the Negro lying in the swamp with his face blown off,
and in northern cities with his manhood maligned and felt the writhing
of his viscera like that of the hare hunted down or the bear at bay,
and I saw men working and taking no joy in their work
and embracing the hard-eyed whore with joyless excitement
and lying with wives and virgins in impotence.

And as I groped in darkness
and felt the pain of millions,
gradually, like day driving night across the continent,
I saw dawn upon them like the sun a vision
of a time when all men walk proudly through the earth
and the bombs and missiles lie at the bottom of the ocean
like the bones of dinosaurs buried under the shale of eras,
and men strive with each other not for power or the accumulation of paper
but in joy create for others the house, the poem, the game of athletic beauty.

Then washed in the brightness of this vision,
I saw how in its radiance would grow and be nourished and suddenly
burst into terrible and splendid bloom
the blood-red flower of revolution.

[1948]

Randall at his typewriter. (Photo by Hugh Grannum, courtesy of the *Detroit Free Press*)

IMAGES FROM BLACK BOTTOM

The Black Aesthetic in the Thirties, Forties, and Fifties

Every poet is molded by his age, by the great events or Great Event that took place during his impressionable years. In the thirties it was the Great Depression and the Spanish Civil War. In the forties it was World War II. In the fifties it was McCarthyism, the Korean War, and the beginning of the Freedom movement with the Supreme Court school-desegregation decision of 1954.

Some poets, such as Langston Hughes and Arna Bontemps, lived from the Negro Renaissance through the post-Renaissance period into the period of the Black Aesthetic and black power of the sixties. Others, like Gwendolyn Brooks and Robert Hayden, published their first books in the forties and are still creating. I shall describe these later poets only as they wrote in the middle period between the Renaissance and the Black Aesthetic, as their further development does not come within the scope of this essay.

During this middle period, and previously during the Harlem Renaissance, there was no such concept as a black aesthetic. Negro writers wanted to be accepted into the mainstream of American literature. The closest thing to a black aesthetic was Langston Hughes's declaration in "The Negro Artist and the Racial Mountain" (1926). He wrote:

> One of the most promising of the young Negro poets said to me once, "I want to be a poet—not a Negro poet," meaning, I believe, "I want to write like a white poet"; meaning subconsciously, "I would like to be a white poet"; meaning behind that, "I would like to be white."
>
> And I was sorry the young man said that, for no great poet has ever been afraid of being himself. And I doubted then that, with his desire to run away spiritually from his race, this boy would ever be a great poet. But this is the mountain standing in the way of any true Negro art in America—this urge within the race toward whiteness, the desire to pour racial individuality into the mold of American standardization, and to be as little Negro and as much American as possible.

Hughes went on to state: "But, to my mind, it is the duty of the younger Negro artist, if he accepts any duty at all from outsiders, to change through the force of his art that old whispering 'I want to be white,' hidden in the aspirations of his people, to 'Why should I want to be white? I am a Negro—and beautiful!'"

This is as close to the Black Aesthetic cry of "I'm black, and beautiful!" as it is possible to come.

Hughes continued: "So I am ashamed for the black poet who says, 'I want to be a poet, not a Negro poet,' as though his own racial world were not as interesting as any other world." Hughes concluded with the oft-quoted declaration:

> We younger Negro artists who create now intend to express our individual dark-skinned selves without fear or shame. If white people are pleased, we are glad. If they are not, it doesn't matter. We know we are beautiful. And ugly too. The tom-tom cries and the tom-tom laughs. If colored people are pleased, we are glad. If they are not, their displeasure doesn't matter either. We build our temple for tomorrow, strong as we know how, and we stand on top of the mountain, free within ourselves.

This sounds much like the Black Aesthetic credo, but there are significant points of difference. For instance, Hughes uses the word Negro. Some Negro ideologues have forbidden Negroes to call Negroes Negroes. Hughes stresses individualism ("express our individual dark-skinned selves"). In the Black Aesthetic, individualism is frowned upon. Feedback from black people, or the mandates of self-appointed literary commissars, is supposed to guide the poet. But Hughes says, "If colored people are pleased we are glad. If they are not, their displeasure doesn't matter either." (Another expression of individualism.) Hughes says, "We know we are beautiful. And ugly too." In the Black Aesthetic, Negroes are always beautiful.

In my own opinion, this feedback usually comes from the most vocal group, ideologues or politicians, who are eager to use the persuasiveness of literature to seize or consolidate power for themselves. Politicians such as Stalin or Khrushchev have a certain low cunning, but they cannot grasp the complexity or paradoxes of life and literature, and they try to impose their own simplemindedness and conformity upon them.

The Great Event of the 1930s was the Depression. In contrast to the affluent 1960s, poverty was everywhere. Millionaires as well as poor people lost everything. Everyone was in this catastrophe together. Eyes were turned toward Russia and communism, and the Communists were active in organizing rent strikes, labor unions, and campaigns for relief. Federal Writers' Projects were started, where black and white authors worked together. Even if black writers did not join the Communist Party, as did Richard Wright, they were sympathetic toward it and its policy of non-discrimination. Black writers did not give up their struggle for Negro rights, but regarded it as part of the struggle for the rights of man everywhere. A popular union organizing slogan was "Black and white, unite and fight."

Robert Hayden wrote his "Speech," in which he urged black and white workers to cooperate:

I have seen the hand
Holding the blowtorch
To the dark, anguish-twisted body;
I have seen the hand
Giving the high-sign
To fire on the white pickets;
And it was the same hand,
Brothers, listen to me,
It was the same hand.

The horizons of poets were widened beyond their own Negro struggle to include world events. In his first book, *Heart-Shape in the Dust,* Hayden wrote of youths dying in the Spanish Civil War, in "Spring Campaign":

She wears a gas mask, fair Corinna does,
And she thinks of spring's first air raid while
    Seeking spring's first rose.

In the same book (1940), he foretold the death of Adolph Hitler, in "Prophecy":

He fell with his mouth
Crushing into the cold earth
And lay unharming at last
Under the falling leaves and the fog. . . .

They returned to the ruined city
And began to build again.

Hayden's second book, *A Ballad of Remembrance,* was not published until 1962, but in the meantime there were the brochures *The Lion and the Archer* (with Myron O'Higgins, 1948) and *Figure of Time* (1955), published in his own "Counterpoise Series." The surrealistic *A Ballad of Remembrance* is chilling with its whirling, glittering images and rhythms and its feeling of nightmare and irrationality. It captures the black experience, but filtered through the poet's sensitive subjectivity:

Accommodate, muttered the Zulu king, throned
Like a copper toad in a glaucous poison jewel.
Love, chimed the saints and the angels and the mermaids
Hate, shrieked the gunmetal priestess
From her spiked bell collar curved like a fleur-de-lys!

As well have a talon as a finger, a muzzle
as a mouth. As well have a hollow as a heart.
And she pinwheeled away in coruscations
of laughter, scattering those others before her.

In "Middle Passage" and "Runagate Runagate," Hayden incorporates all the innovations of the experimental poets of the 1920s: varied and expressive rhythms; anti-poetic materials such as quotations from handbills, legal documents, ships' logs; scraps of poetry, hymns, spirituals; fusing all these together to make two exciting narratives of the beginning and of the escape from slavery.

Gwendolyn Brooks, in *A Street in Bronzeville* (1945), wrote of the black people on the South Side of Chicago, but world events widened her vision to include also sonnets of black men at war. In her Pulitzer prize-winning *Annie Allen* (1949), she uses many poetic forms with easy mastery, from ballads to crisp sonnets:

What shall I give my children? Who are poor,
Who are adjudged the leastwise of the land,
Who are my sweetest lepers, who demand
No velvet and no velvety velour. . . .

In the tight, seven-lined trochaic stanzas of *The Anniad,* she deftly balances narrative, images, and rhythm:

Leads her to a lonely room
Which she makes a chapel of.
Where she genuflects to love.
All the prayer books in her eyes
Open soft as sacrifice
Or the dolor of a dove.
Tender candles ray by ray
Warm and gratify the gray.

Like Tolson and Hayden, she has the long poem firmly in control.

Langston Hughes continued to write of black urban folk, but now he abandoned the glamour of night clubs and of a Harlem pandering to white seekers of thrills. He wrote of the maids, porters, and laborers of Harlem instead of the dancers, singers, and "lean-headed jazzers" of the cabarets. His series on "Madame Alberta K. Washington" presents with humor a strong-minded Negro domestic worker.

He still wrote on racial themes, but he wrote within the context of democracy for all. The Negro struggle was a part of the world-wide struggle for freedom. This universality is expressed in "I Dream a World":

A world I dream where black or white,
Whatever race you be,
Will share the bounties of the earth
And every man is free.

In his poems, instances of injustice are ironically juxtaposed with the American Dream or with American ideals, as in his poem "Freedom Train." An unsolvable dilemma is presented in his "Merry-Go-Round," where a Negro child asks in frustration, where is the back of the merry-go-round, as black people always have to sit at the back.

The very title of M. B. Tolson's book *Rendezvous with America* (1944) suggests a widening of the poet's interest. He writes from the point of view of the Negro, but he has expanding sympathy with other ethnic groups, shown in his title poem.

A blind man said,
"Look at the kikes,"
And I saw
Rosenwald sowing the seeds of culture in the Black Belt. . . .
A blind man said,
"Look at the Chinks,"
And I saw
Lin Yutang crying the World Charter in the white man's
wilderness. . . .

In this book, Tolson uses a wide variety of poetry forms, from rhymed quatrains and sonnets to long poems written in varying measures. He shows his architectonic power in building long poems that do not bore the reader, foreshadowing his mastery of longer forms in *Libretto for the Republic of Liberia* and *Harlem Gallery.* His sonnets are dramatic—compressing narrative, characterization, theme, and dramatic tension into fourteen lines. Perhaps his most successful sonnet is "Incident at Versailles," with its succinct characterization of Clemenceau, Lloyd George, and Wilson, and its implicit prophecy of all the future disasters that were to spring from the racism of these world leaders. In general, the language of the poems is vigorous, although it is sometimes marred by clichés and archaic syntax.

In 1953 he published *Libretto for the Republic of Liberia,* a long poem commissioned for the centennial of the African nation, which earned him the title of Poet Laureate of Liberia. The preface was written by Allen Tate, and appeared also in *Poetry* magazine, with an excerpt from the book.

In his preface, Tate said that Tolson had for the first time incorporated the modern poetic language into a poem written by a Negro. In this poem, Tolson used all the devices dear to the New Criticism: recondite allusions, scraps of foreign languages, African proverbs, symbolism, objective correlatives. Many parts of the poem are obscure, not through some private symbolism of the author, but because of the unusual words, foreign phrases, and learned allusions. If the reader has a well-stored mind, or is willing to use dictionaries, encyclopedias, atlases, and other reference books, the poem should present no great difficulty. Reading this poem is like reading other learned poets, such as Milton and T. S. Eliot.

The history of the poem is interesting. Tolson sent the manuscript to Tate, who returned it. Then Tolson rewrote the poem according to the tenets of the

New Criticism. The irony is that, about this time, the New Criticism was declining, and the Beat poets, with their looser, freer, more emotional language and form, were coming into popularity. In any case, the learned allusive language is not the spontaneous speech of the Negro people.

Hayden, Brooks, and Tolson can be grouped together as poets conscious of technique, who were familiar with and learned from the modern experimental masters such as Hart Crane, Eliot, Pound, and Yeats, and not from minor poets such as Houseman or Edna St. Vincent Millay, or traditional poets such as Keats, all of whom influenced Countee Cullen.

They were conscious of their Negro race, but they regarded it in the wider context of a world-wide depression and a world-wide war against fascism. Their world view was wider and more inclusive than that of the Renaissance poets.

Other poets, perhaps not more conscious of race, but in whose work race occupies a more central position, were Sterling Brown, Margaret Walker, and Frank Marshall Davis.

Sterling Brown was in the same age group as the Renaissance poets, but his sole collection of poetry, *Southern Road,* was published in 1932. In this book, the influence of Negro folk poetry, of spirituals, blues, and ballads, is evident. Like Langston Hughes, he brings the blues stanza into formal verse. He has the unusual and valuable quality of humor, which permeates his ballads of Slim Greer, a picaresque adventurer. There are ballads of John Henry and of the chain gang, and poems of sharecroppers and southern rural life. These are poems of Negro life written out of black experience grounded in folk poetry which he intensifies with his art.

Margaret Walker, born in Jackson, Mississippi, is also influenced by Negro folk poetry. In her only volume of poetry, *For My People,* published in 1942 in the Yale University Series of Younger Poets, there are ballads of rural southern folk, of the witch Molly Means, of "Bad-man Stagolee" and "Big John Henry."

Unlike Brown, however, whose poems not in the folk tradition and folk forms were apt to be personal and subjective, Walker used the classical sonnet form (sometimes without rhyme) to write about Negroes. The sonnet about miners and sharecroppers titled "Childhood," and the one titled "The Struggle Staggers Us" are outstanding in this series.

Ours is a struggle from a too-warm bed;
too cluttered with a patience full of sleep.

Out of this blackness we must struggle forth;
from want of bread, of pride, of dignity.

More experimental than Brown, and probably influenced by Carl Sandburg, she wrote some poems in long free-verse paragraphs like those of Fenton Johnson. The most famous of these is the title poem, "For My People." This poem gains its force not by tropes—turns of language or thought—or logical development of a theme, but by the sheer overpowering accumulation of a mass of details delivered in rhythmical parallel phrases. "We Have Been Believers" is another powerful poem in a similar form and on a racial theme.

Race is central also in Frank Marshall Davis's book *Black Man's Verse, I Am the American Negro,* and *47th Street.*

A Chicago poet, he is inspired not by traditional Negro folk poetry, as are Brown and Walker, but by the teeming black life of a northern metropolis. His free verse shows the influence of Sandburg and Masters. In "Giles Johnson Ph.D." and "Robert Whitmore," he satirizes the pretensions of the black bourgeoisie. In the labor-organizing thirties, he wrote of sharecroppers and labor unions. His poetry is black-centered, without the focus on wider horizons found in the poetry of Hayden and Tolson.

Fenton Johnson was another poet who wrote in free verse influenced by Carl Sandburg. His earlier poetry was romantic, conventional, and traditional. In his later poetry he adopted the long free-verse line-strophe of Sandburg, and wrote poems expressing his disillusionment with America. Although marred by clichés and conventional expressions such as "fallen woman," they are new and different in their mood of frustration and despair.

These poets exemplify the trends of the thirties, forties, and fifties. There was a world depression and a world war. In their outlook, black poets saw race as one problem among the world problems of poverty and fascism, and appealed to all men of goodwill to help solve the problem. As for their style, they no longer considered it sufficient to pour new wine of content into old bottles of form but absorbed the techniques of the experimental poets Hart Crane, Pound, and Eliot. In this group were Tolson, Hayden, and Brooks. Another group—Brown, Walker, Davis, and Fenton Johnson—were influenced in varying degrees by Negro folk poetry and by Sandburg and Masters. Race was central in their poetry. Langston Hughes, growing beyond the Renaissance attraction to the more superficial and merely picturesque aspects of Negro life, wrote of its more serious aspects in the speech of the urban working man and in blues and jazz cadences.

There was no consciously formulated Black Aesthetic. Black poets considered themselves as part of American literature, although most of them were excluded from textbooks, anthologies, and, to a great extent, from magazines. It remains to be seen whether, in our time, the Black Aesthetic will stimulate superior poetry. The proof will have to be in the poems produced.

However, I will not hedge in caution, but will be imprudent enough to weigh the historical facts, note the trends, and make a prediction.

In the forties, black poets absorbed the innovations of white poets. In future years, they will not only absorb them, but will transcend them, and create their own innovations. Both Don Lee and Amiri Baraka are well-read, but they and poets like them will not only absorb what they've read but, using their heritage of folk poetry and black music, will build something new upon that. In short, they'll do their own thing. They will not depend upon white publishers, white audiences, or white critics, as there are black publishers, black critics, and an increasing black audience. Robert Hayden and Gwendolyn Brooks are mature and at the height of their powers, and are capable of change and growth. There are many younger poets not yet even published in book form. All that I can foresee is a poetry of increasing power and richness, which will make a glorious contribution to the world.

[1970]

Old Witherington

Old Witherington had drunk too much again.
The children changed their play and packed around him
To jeer his latest brawl. Their parents followed.

Prune-black, with bloodshot eyes and one white tooth.
He tottered in the night with legs spread wide
Waving a hatchet. "Come on, come on," he piped.
"And I'll baptize these bricks with bloody kindling.
I may be old and drunk, but not afraid
To die. I've died before. A million times
I've died and gone to hell. I live in hell.
If I die now I die, and put an end
To all this loneliness. Nobody cares
Enough to even fight me now, except
This crazy bastard here."

                              And with these words
He cursed the little children, cursed his neighbors,
Cursed his father, mother, and his wife,
Himself, and God, and all the rest of the world,
All but his grinning adversary, who, crouched,
Danced tenderly around him with a jag-toothed bottle.
As if the world compressed to one old man
Who was the sun, and he sole faithful planet.

[1943]

For Pharish Pinckney, Bindle-Stiff during the Depression

You'd wake at morning, stiff from the hard floor
of rattling box car in a swaying train,
and wave at girls you'd never seen before
in little towns you'd never see again.

You felt the joy of roaming far and free,
and in the jungle shared the hobo's stew,
and learned the kindness and the cruelty
of the land that mothered and rejected you.

Now, in the land you loved and cursed, you sleep.
Summer and winter lave you with their tears.
Fruitless to ask now, Do you smile or weep?
Your bitter laugh no longer rives our ears.
 In the womb you left to suffer and to die,
 Find peace at last, while you in silence lie.

[1949]
[May 1981]

47

Vacant Lot

Crouched in its giant green the Indian hid
And on the trapper sprang the ambuscade.
It was the wilderness to city kid,
And paradise to each pariah weed.

We'd give the slip to megaphone-voiced wardens
For atavistic field where memories blur,
As asters make their getaway from gardens
And scrape acquaintance with the uncultured burr.

There, amid sunflowers, goldenrod, and thistle,
We acted the old drama of boys' strength,
Bloodied each other's noses, and would wrestle
Till hustled home to bed by moon at length.

While April set us sprinting round the bases,
October chasing the eccentric ball,
December sculpturing farcical forms and faces,
It was chameleon stage containing all.

[1942]

Ghetto Girls

(Originally titled "Hastings Street Girls")

With ivory, saffron, cinnamon, chocolate faces,
Glowing with all the hues of all the races;
Lips laughing, generous-curved, vermilion-tinted,
Lips of a child, but, like a woman's painted;
Eyes where the morning stars yet glimmer on;
Feet swift to dance through juke-box nights till dawn:

> *O little girls, so young, so foolish-wise,*
> *Flaunting such knowledge in your ignorant eyes,*
> *You are like flowers that bud, then droop away,*
> *Or like the bright, quick-darkened tropic day.*
> *Lovers and kisses, cruel, careless, light,*
> *Will you remember down the long, deep night?*

[1937, 1967]

Laughter in the Slums

In crippled streets where happiness seems buried
under the sooty snow of northern winter,
sudden as bells at twilight,
bright as the moon, full as the sun, there blossoms
in southern throats rich flower of flush fields
hot with the furnace sun of Georgia Junes,
laughter that cold and blizzards could not kill.

[1937]

George

When I was a boy desiring the title of man
And toiling to earn it
In the inferno of the foundry knockout,
I watched and admired you working by my side,
As, goggled, with mask on your mouth and shoulders bright with sweat,
You mastered the monstrous, lumpish cylinder blocks.
And when they clotted the line and plunged to the floor
With force enough to tear your foot in two,
You calmly stepped aside.

One day when the line broke down and the blocks reared up
Groaning, grinding, and mounted like an ocean wave
And then rushed thundering down like an avalanche,
And we frantically dodged, then braced our heads together
To form an arch to lift and stack them,
You gave me your highest accolade:
You said: "You not afraid of sweat. You strong as a mule."

Now, here, in the hospital,
In a ward where old men wait to die,
You sit, and watch time go by.
You cannot read the books I bring, not even
Those that are only picture books,
As you sit among the senile wrecks,
The psychopaths, the incontinent.

One day when you fell from your chair and stared at the air
With the look of fright which sight of death inspires,
I lifted you like a cylinder block, and said,
"Don't be afraid
Of a little fall, for you'll be here
A long time yet, because you're strong as a mule."

[1964]

A Cup for the Loser

What Papa liked to do most of all was to argue. He never called it arguing, but always discussing, but anyway to me it sounded just like plain arguing. He used to read the editorial pages and when he found something he agreed with he would read it out loud and exclaim, "Very true, very true!" He would cut out the article and put it in a folder where he kept clippings and would use the reasoning in his next argument, or discussion, as he called it. He would argue about anything—politics, or the Bible, or morals, or history, or sports—anything that a fellow could think of, but mostly he liked to argue about health, and how smoking and drinking undermined your health.

He had never smoked or drunk in his life, and was a fine physical specimen. He was a little under middle height, about five feet six or seven, but was powerfully built, with wide shoulders, a narrow waist and swelling thighs and biceps. He used to boast that when he was in the cavalry he had the largest chest expansion of any man in his regiment. He used to talk about how hard the work was at the foundry, but how even though he was in his forties he could keep working while younger men were falling out all around him.

Anyway, to get back to Papa's arguments, or discussions, the thing he discussed the most and the loudest was the evil of drinking. One reason he discussed it so much was that although those were Prohibition days, the roomers always seemed to find plenty to drink.

Sometimes a roomer would come in drunk and Mama would have to put him to bed. Or sometimes a couple would be drinking and suddenly change from playing and lovey-doveying to quarrelling and breaking up the furniture on each other's heads, and Papa would have to stop the fight and counsel them about drinking. So he was constantly discussing the drinking habit with them, since it was hard on his own property as well as on their health.

Maybe the biggest discussion he had about drinking was with old Mr. Goodlow, the inventor. Mr. Goodlow was a fat man in his fifties who was a janitor (or custodian as he insisted that everyone call him) in some building downtown. He claimed to be an inventor and was always talking about some invention or other and all the money he'd make when they got on the market. He said that when his inventions paid off he'd send me and my brother Jack to college. One invention he did have was a cigar container. He had a sample of it which he carried in his breast pocket and would show to anyone he could back into a corner.

One night Papa had just read aloud an editorial which discussed the findings of some scientists concerning the effects of drinking on the morals and health of the country when Mr. Goodlow walked in carrying a glass jug containing a clear colorless liquid.

"How are you, Papa?" said Mr. Goodlow. All the roomers called him Papa, although he was younger than Mr. Goodlow and some of the others.

"Just fine," said Papa. "How's the invention coming?"

"It's looking up, it's looking up," said Mr. Goodlow. "Before long every cigar smoker in the country will be carrying his butts in Goodlow's Sanitary Cigar Container. I had a promising consultation with my lawyer this afternoon, and I brought home a little something to celebrate." He lifted up the jug.

Papa raised his eyebrows and stared at the jug. At first he must have thought it was kerosene for the oil stove, as no roomer had ever dared to bring liquor openly in the house. Besides, he and Mr. Goodlow had had several arguments about drinking and Mr. Goodlow knew how Papa felt about it. I guess he didn't understand Papa very well, and thought he could change his mind by arguing.

"Mr. Goodlow," said Papa, in a grieved tone, "You don't tell me that that's liquor in that jug you're carrying."

"Yes, sir," said Mr. Goodlow with dignity. "It's the best custom-made white mule I've ever tasted. I had to pay five dollars a gallon for it."

"Mr. Goodlow," said Papa. "You were just saying that your invention was about to be a success. What a pity it would be if before you could enjoy your success your mind was deranged and your body debilitated by that—that poison."

Mr. Goodlow drew himself up proudly and said, "I guess my mind is equal to yours and though you're a younger man I don't think my body is any inferior."

He looked very dignified with his white hair and mustache showing up against his black skin, and his generous belly bulging against his vest made him look like a Bishop or a prosperous policy man.

"Why, right here in the paper it says how scientists have proved that whiskey is bad for your health. You can't contradict that," said Papa.

"I can contradict anything," said Mr. Goodlow. "I've been drinking all my life. The more I drink, the healthier I get. I don't pay any attention to what some fanatic bluenose says who's afraid to enjoy life and doesn't want anybody else to enjoy it either."

That made Papa angry, for what he hated most of all was to be called a fanatic or accused of being afraid of anything. He raised his voice and began waving his arms and pounding his fist as if he were making a speech. He went and got his folder and produced articles to show how harmful drinking was. He quoted from the Bible.

Mr. Goodlow was not an ignorant man, and for every argument Papa put forth he had an answering one. For every quotation from the Bible against drinking he could produce one in favor of it. They made so much noise that Jack came from upstairs and he and I giggled in enjoyment, and Mama came from the kitchen and said, "Papa, what are you making all that noise for? You'll have everybody in the house and the neighborhood complaining."

What made Mr. Goodlow mad was Papa's referring to his age and telling him how dangerous it was for a man of his years to drink. Finally he said, "I'm an older man than you are, but I bet I can out-run you anytime, just to prove that drinking doesn't hurt me. You talk so much about being scientific. You and I can prove this right now by making an experiment."

Papa answered right quick, "All right. We'll race on the schoolyard. And if I win you'll have to admit that drinking has ruined your health."

"I won't have to admit anything, because I'll win. But we can make a little bet on this. If I win, you'll have to take a drink with me."

Papa frowned. He didn't believe in betting. "I'm not a betting man. We don't have to bet to settle this anyway."

"Oh, it won't really be a bet. There won't be any money changing hands. We'll call it a penalty. I'll tell you what I'll do. If you win, I'll—I'll quit drinking, er, I'll quit drinking—er, for a week."

"Make it a month," said Papa, "and I'll take it. When you see how well you feel after one month, you won't want to drink any more after that."

"All right," said Mr. Goodlow. "I could make it a year, because I know I'll win."

By this time Jack and I were dancing around with anticipation. Mr. Goodlow took off his coat and took a big swig of the white mule. He belched and sweat broke out on his face.

"The way I feel now, I could out-run Man O'War," he said.

Papa looked at him and shook his head. "You shouldn't kill your chances of winning like that," he said. "After all, I want to win in a fair contest, not with my opponent disabled before he starts."

Mr. Goodlow snorted. "Come on, let's go. I feel like a kid again."

As we passed through the kitchen to go out the back door to the school yard, Mama said, "Papa, where are you going?"

"Mr. Goodlow and I are going to race to settle a little argument we had."

"Don't you go disgrace yourself running on the street like a wild man. Who ever heard of such a thing? You'll be the laughingstock of the neighborhood."

"I don't care who laughs as long as I prove I'm right. We won't be long."

Papa, Mr. Goodlow, Jack and I cut through the back yard and climbed over the fence to the school yard. Jack and I climbed over nimbly. Papa didn't have much trouble getting over, but he had to pull Mr. Goodlow over from the other side. His big stomach got caught on the top of the fence and Papa had to jerk him to get him over and he almost fell on his face on the other side.

It was an autumn night. The moon and the street lamps made the yard fairly bright. It stretched still and silvery to the schoolhouse about seventy-five yards away. It was cool and pleasant, and a few neighbors were sitting on their porches on the other side of the street. When they saw two men and two boys enter the playground in such an unusual way, there was a stir among the light-colored shirts and dresses, but no one came over.

Papa began to do bending exercises, to raise his knees high in the air and to run back and forth, the way runners do at track meets.

"What's he doing all that for?" said Mr. Goodlow.

"That's to warm up," I said, "So he can run faster."

"I don't need to warm up," said Mr. Goodlow. "That mule made me plenty warm."

After Papa had warmed up he started digging two holes in the ground for his toes. Mr. Goodlow looked at them suspiciously. "What are those for?" he demanded.

"That's to give you a faster start," said Papa. "Aren't you going to make any?"

"No," said Mr. Goodlow. "That's too much bending down."

"If you won't use any, I won't either," said Papa. "Let's race to that concrete walk leading to the schoolhouse. It's about seventy-five or eighty yards away. Can you run that far?"

"I can run a mile if I feel like it," snorted Mr. Goodlow.

"Jack," said Papa, "You go to the walk and see who reaches it first. Dave, you stay here and start us off."

He turned to Mr. Goodlow. "Now it's agreed that if I win, you quit drinking any kind of liquor for one month. If you win, I'll take a drink with you."

"That's our agreement," said Mr. Goodlow.

"All right, Dave," said Papa. "Start us off."

Papa and Mr. Goodlow were standing side by side facing the walk, each with one leg outstretched. Papa was slim, but powerfully built, and looked like a real athlete, although he did seem old to me, in my childhood years. Mr. Goodlow was breathing heavily and was sweating. His big stomach made his shirt stick out. His thick neck hung over his open collar. It seemed a cinch that Papa would win the race.

"On your marks!" I said. "Get set! Go!"

Mr. Goodlow was slow in starting, but Papa was off in a flash, with his body bent forward and his arms working powerfully. Mr. Goodlow puffed and labored, but the distance between him and Papa increased so rapidly that he seemed to be moving backward. Before Papa reached the halfway mark he was three yards ahead of Mr. Goodlow.

"Come on, Fats!" somebody called from across the street. "You can't win like that."

Papa was drawing farther and farther ahead of Mr. Goodlow. But he never slowed up or looked back. On the contrary, he made a final spurt as he neared the finish, but his feet slipped on the gravel and he fell headlong on the ground. He must have been stunned for a few seconds, for he lay still while Mr. Goodlow lumbered past him. He rose to his knees, shook his head, pulled himself to his feet, and began to run after Mr. Goodlow. The finish was so close that from where I was, running along behind them, I couldn't tell who had won. Mr. Goodlow was leaning against the schoolhouse, panting.

"Who won, Jack? Who won?" cried Papa.

"I don't know," said Jack. "It was close I couldn't hardly tell."

"Speak up, boy," said Papa. "One of us had to win. Who reached the finish line first?"

"Well, I guess Mr. Goodlow did," said Jack. "His stomach stuck out across the walk just ahead of you."

Mr. Goodlow staggered to Jack and clapped him on the back. "You're a sharp-eyed boy," he said. "I won by a nose. That proves that the race is to him who endures unto the end."

"But I fell down," said Papa. "We'll have to race over again."

"That's not my fault," said Mr. Goodlow. "I had a shot of whiskey, and I didn't fall down. If you fall down in a race, that's just your bad luck. You know that. Now come on to the house and take your medicine."

Papa opened his mouth to protest, but suddenly clamped his teeth tight so that the muscles on his jaws stood out. He turned and strode back to the house.

"Come over here, David," said Mr. Goodlow. He puts his arms on Jack's and my shoulders, and leaned on us, wheezing and grunting, as we walked back to the house. Jack and I looked at each other questioningly, wondering what Papa was going to do.

We didn't climb over the fence this time, but walked slowly to the side gate. When we entered the kitchen, Papa was waiting, and Mama was watching him with a sort of smile in her eyes.

Mr. Goodlow said, "I've been thinking about the race. Let's call the whole thing off. I was reserving my strength for a spurt at the finish, but since you fell down I didn't need to use it. We don't know whether I would have won or not. So let's forget about the bet."

"I lost, and I'll pay," said Papa. "But I'm not going to take a drink in front of my children. Take that jug upstairs to your room."

Mama, Jack and I listened to the door slam. We heard the men walk upstairs, and in a minute we heard the clink of glasses and Mr. Goodlow's laughter. We looked at each other. We hardly knew what to think. For Papa to take a drink, after talking against drinking for so many years, was almost as if the sky had fallen down.

Then we heard Papa walking downstairs. He stamped into the kitchen with his lips clamped, grabbed a glass from the sink, dipped it into the dishpan and gulped down the dishwater. Then he went into the bathroom and we could hear him getting rid of the whiskey.

"It's time you children went to bed," said Mama. She said it so sternly that we didn't fool around, but went straight to bed. Our room was next to Mr. Goodlow's, and we could hear him rattling glasses, smacking his lips, belching and chuckling. We whispered about the race until we fell asleep.

However, even though Papa took a drink on that occasion, that was the only time I knew him to do so. After that he never argued about drinking, and never tried to persuade anyone not to drink.

[1947]

Victoria

"But something kept him rooted here, like a spectator at a play who identifies himself with the actors, and is involved in the action."

David was happy. He was waiting for Victoria, to ask her a question, and if she gave him the answer he expected, he would be happier still. He had played in the schoolyard all afternoon, and when he had enough of play he came up to his den in the attic.

His den was at the end of the attic near the one small window level with the floor. His desk was an old army blanket spread on the floor, his bookcase an egg crate containing his books and notebooks.

The window overlooked the playground which extended from his backyard to the school near the other end of the block. He swung it open, admitting the freshness of the April afternoon and the voices of the children on the schoolyard.

David's glance wandered over the field flooded with sunshine. A group of boys and a group of girls were playing baseball, and smaller children were climbing on the swing supports and horizontal bars. Near the alley, some older youths were playing dice, with one on the lookout for the roaches. The bright shirts and dresses, the movements of the ball players, the crack of bats on balls and the shouts of the players made the field a world of color and motion and sound.

David projected himself into the scene. He was striking the ball, running the bases. He was crouched in the corner over the dice, caressing them and talking to them like a lover. While he was immersed in these actions he was aware of another self that stood aloof and watched him doing these things, and of yet another self that watched him watching himself, like a series of mirrors.

David did not see Victoria on the playground, and he began to write in his notebook:

In the spring of his seventeenth year David first saw her, And fell in love with her. She was playing with other girls, but she was the only one he saw. She out-hit and out-ran and out-laughed them all. She was tall and lithe and shapely. Her arms and legs were bare, and darkened by the sun to the color of bronze. Her voice was like the sound of silver.

That was how he first saw Victoria. He learned her name from his friends and asked his big sister about her. Rachel laughed.

"Are you carrying a torch for Victoria? What do you see in her? She's box-ankled and wall-eyed."

"She has big eyes and pretty legs." David paid no attention to Rachel. She was laughing at him only because he was interested in a different girl from the ones she was always trying to put off on him, and in whom he was never interested.

Rachel told him that Victoria was an orphan. She lived with her uncle and her aunt, who made her do all the housework but let her come and go as she pleased after she had done her work.

David learned all these things about her before he ever spoke to her. One day as he was shambling along the street with his eyes cast down to avoid stumbling on the level pavement, he saw a pair of small feet, then a pair of brown legs. He did not know whose they were, but there was something familiar and exciting about them. Looking up, he saw Victoria coming toward him. There was no one whom he would rather have met, yet he began thinking of ways to avoid her. He looked about wildly. But he had passed the alley and had not reached the cross street. He could turn into a doorway or cross to the other side of the street, but that would be too obvious. He could pass her without speaking, but that was rude. But if he spoke to her first, would she answer him? Now she was upon him. What could he do? She smiled, and said, "Hello, David."

David grew dizzy and faint and thought he was going to fall on the street. He put out his hand as if to clutch at something and stammered, "H-hello." After she passed, he leaned against a telephone pole until he was able to walk again.

After that he would speak to her whenever they met. He made no attempt to seek her out or to go the places where she might be. He was content with occasional chance meetings. They made his days rich and adventuresome. Who could tell when and where he would see her, he would speak to her, she would smile at him and utter his name? Always the same thing happened to him. The blood rushed to his face, his knees grew weak, he became dizzy and could hardly speak. He would make his way back home giddy and excited and would write an account of the meeting.

About this time he became acquainted with Dante's love poetry in *The New Life*. It expressed his emotions perfectly. Dante's chance meetings with Beatrice and his adoration of her were just like his encounters with Victoria and his love for her. He read them incessantly and learned *The New Life* almost by heart. He bought an Italian grammar and a book of Italian poetry and read Dante's love poems in the original.

Things might have gone on like this indefinitely if he had not had a talk with Ned Adams. David liked to go to the settlement house sometimes to work out with the boxers. One night Ned Adams, who was the city amateur middleweight champion, asked him to go a couple of rounds with him. David shook Ned twice with rights to the head. The champion could have hurt him in retaliation, but good-naturedly refrained. He smothered David with left hooks and looping rights to the head, but his blows had no more sharpness than the sheathed paws of a playful kitten.

When they were dressing Ned looked him up and down and said, "You're built like a fighter. You have a punch like a mule and are fast as hell. Why don't you train regular? In two years we could make a champion out of you."

A lightweight on the next bench laughed. "He's too busy chasing tail."

David said hotly, "I can't be bothered with girls. They get in my hair."

Ned looked at him skeptically. He was older than David, about twenty. "Maybe you don't have the right line. Girls like to be courted. You can't stand off and expect them to come to you. You have to go to them. I know that girls can't talk sense like you can talk to another guy. You have to give them a lot of bull. Tell 'em they're pretty and crap like that. They'll eat it up. And there's another thing. You have to play each one different. I'm fooling around with a little fox that's trying to play hard to get. I've been giving her the absent line. I haven't been around for two or three weeks. When I do show up, she'll be ready to fall into my lap."

Victoria is not like that, David thought. Nevertheless, Ned's words made him think of getting better acquainted with her. So far he had been content to admire her from a distance. This feeling had come on him so suddenly that he had not had time to adjust to it. He was not sure what he would do, but he vaguely imagined that some time in the future Victoria would be his girl. Now he began to think of some practical means of winning her. He made up his mind that the next time he met her, instead of merely saying hello he would stop and talk with her and learn to know her better.

The very next day when he walked into Mr. Siegel's drugstore he saw her standing by the counter. He was totally unprepared for the meeting. At least when he met her on the street he had some seconds of preparation before speaking to her. Now he was totally surprised. He could hardly stand, so he dropped upon a stool at the soda fountain. Victoria smiled at him. Thinking of things to say, he forgot to say anything.

Mr. Siegel said, "What'll it be, David?"

Mechanically he blurted out, "I'll take a soda." Then suddenly to Victoria, "Won't you have one with me?"

"No, thanks, I just had one."

His heart sank.

She hesitated. "But I wouldn't mind another one."

She sat down by his side. They began to talk of school and of neighborhood events. David had often dreamed of some day talking to wise men and poets, but even in his imagination those conversations were not so exciting as the one with Victoria. She was easy to talk with, and gradually David became outwardly calm. But all the while the air seemed shaking with some tremendous music of organ or full orchestra, to which his heart, blood and pulse danced riotously.

He never knew what they said, but he noticed how long, black and curly her hair was, and how it poured upon her shoulders. Her eyebrows were straight and thick, the lashes long and glossy. Her eyes were large and soft, her nose delicately chiseled. Her skin was copper-colored, and her cheek, suffused with red, had the gentle curves of a child's.

After she finished her soda she stood up and said, "Thank you for the soda. I enjoyed it."

As she walked out he noticed the way her waist tapered from her shoulders and breasts. He sat with his head on his hands thinking about her. At last Mr. Siegel said, "David, does anything hurt you?"

David started up without a word and walked out.

For the next two days David lived in the memory of those moments. Then he began to miss Victoria. He watched for her from the window, looked for her in the streets, and even walked past her house, but he did not see her. One day Rachel found him sitting moodily in front of the window and said, "David, why are you sitting by the window looking half dead? Holy Pete, if you like Victoria, why don't you go out and get her instead of mooning in front of the window and reading those silly books?"

"But what can I do? She's never invited me to her house."

"I wouldn't invite you to my house, either, if I were Victoria. In the first place, why don't you get rid of that sloppy sweatshirt and those baggy pants and change to a shirt and tie. And then get some *savoir-faire*."

"Is that what those over-dressed dim-wits that come to see you are sup-posed to have?"

"At least they're more polished than you, my shabby bookworm. But listen to me. I'm trying to help you. If you want Victoria to be your girl, you'll have to go out and get her. Faint heart never won fair lady. Why don't you invite her to go out with you?"

"But where could I take her?"

"There are lots of places—movies, picnics, dances. I know just the thing. My club's giving a dance next month. You can invite her to that for a start. I'll give you an invitation."

"But how can I take her to a dance? You know I can't dance."

"I'll teach you. You have weeks to learn. Come on. Let's get busy right away."

Rachel put a record on the phonograph and began to show David the basic steps. After he learned them she had him dance with her.

"Don't stand so far away. I won't bite you. I'm your sister. Now relax. Let yourself go, and don't be so wooden, and for heaven's sake don't look so mad. You're not in a gym."

At the end of his first lesson David had made definite progress. He danced every day with Rachel and practiced by himself. Often he was stiff and self-conscious, but sometimes he forgot himself in the music and Rachel would look at him in surprise and say, "You're doing fine. Victoria will enjoy dancing with you."

Her praise would make him conscious again of what he was doing. He would look at his feet and think of the steps and then Rachel would scold him for making mistakes. At the end of a week of daily sessions he thought he had learned enough to invite Victoria to go with him to the dance. Today he was going to invite her. He was waiting until she appeared on the playground. Then he would go outside and speak to her.

He looked out the window again. Behind the roofs were pink and orange clouds. The level sunlight stretched long shadows across the field. Reflected from the red bricks of the street, the light took on a rosy hue. Victoria was not on the field. David reached for his book of Italian poetry and began to read one of Dante's love sonnets.

How wonderfully Dante described Beatrice and the way he felt about her. How wonderful that the description fitted his own girl and himself so perfectly. The poem seemed to be not Dante talking about Beatrice, but himself speaking of Victoria. He would translate it, he would put it into English so she could read it, and at the dance, maybe, he would show it to her.

He turned to a blank page in his notebook and began to write:

My lady carries love within her eyes

How true that was about Victoria. Her eyes were soft and warm and contained nothing but kindness. The first line of a sonnet was always the easiest. Now for the second:

Which renders noble all she looks upon

How true that line was also. For whenever he saw Victoria he felt cleaner and finer. Just as Dante had written *The Divine Comedy* for Beatrice, one day he would write a great poem for Victoria.

The second line of a sonnet was generally easy too. But the third line was where the rimes and the difficulty began:

When she goes by, men turn and gaze at her

That was exactly what happened whenever Victoria walked down the street. For David was not the only one she attracted. When she passed, slim and graceful, with her long black hair hanging over her shoulders, he had seen men turn around and draw in their breath. But that line would not fit. It did not rime with either of the preceding lines.

The thought of her walking down the street reminded David that this was about the time she came to the playground. He glanced out the window. She was there. She wore a plain white dress, like a nurse's, which fit snugly at the waist. She was playing catch with another girl. Two boys stood nearby watching. Now and then they said something to her and they all laughed. She missed the ball and one of the boys turned to retrieve it for her, but she raced him to the ball and picked it up herself. He grabbed her around the waist but she twisted smoothly away from him.

That was one of the things David liked about her. She did not allow anyone to take liberties with her. Even when boys tried to do her favors because she was a girl, she refused to accept them, but kept herself in a position of equality with them. Her refusal was not the curt "I can do anything you can do and better too" of some athletic girls, but a gracious declining that still left them pleased with themselves and with her. She was popular with all the boys and with girls also.

Everything David noticed about her made him like her, and since he stumbled on every curb and every flight of stairs, was ashamed to look into mirrors and could never think of anything to say, he admired her all the more because she was graceful and beautiful and friendly.

Now he would go out and speak to her. Now he would ask her to go to the dance with him and she would consent. He stood up to go, but after taking a step he paused. Suppose she refused? What could he say to persuade her? Until now he had not imagined anything but that she would consent. Now the thought of failure made cold sweat come on his brow. He had better wait a few minutes and think it over. Perhaps he could think of some winning, graceful way to ask her. He picked up the book and lay down again to think.

How clean and fresh she looked. In the museum was the torso of a Greek girl which he loved. The cold white marble seemed to breathe and be soft and warm to the touch. Victoria reminded him of this torso, but with a subtle difference. She had not the antique Greek lines. Her shoulders were wider, her breasts larger, her abdomen flatter and deeper. And she could not be expressed in cold white marble. She was like a statue of bronze, of warm polished bronze with a glaze that gleamed silver in the light above the warm brown metal beneath. There was such a glaze on her skin. He imagined it to be sleek to his fingers.

His attention was diverted to the schoolyard by a sudden movement. Two figures split from the knot of gamblers and walked toward the far end of the yard. David recognized them as Ned Adams and Willie George Lee. Ned wore a close-fitting white rayon polo shirt, blue jeans, and moccasins. He was stocky and barrel-chested but moved easily and lightly.

Willie George was also a boxer—a flyweight, and a tap-dancer as well. He danced in the smaller night clubs. He was older than Ned and one of his cronies. He was dapper as a flea in a lavender sport shirt, green slacks and brown suede shoes.

Ned and Willie George swaggered across the playground. Boys greeted them and girls turned and looked into their faces, but the fighters did not notice them. They stopped a few feet from Victoria. She held the ball in her hand and looked around. Ned stared straight at her. She looked into his eyes. She dropped the ball. Ned picked it up and handed it to her. She smiled. They began to talk.

Meanwhile Willie George accosted the other girl. She was a short plump girl named Eva, whose brother was feeble-minded. David knew her, for one night she came to him and a friend on the schoolyard and asked them to lie down in the doorway of the school with her. The boys stared at each other, hot, flustered. "My father told me to come home," they said in unison, and walked away. Now Willie George seized her by the waist and led her through a dance step. They laughed and applauded themselves.

It was growing darker. The color of the air deepened from rose to violet. One by one or in little groups the boys and girls went home. Their cries and laughter faded away in the dusk. The two couples were alone in the shadows. The street lamps came on. There was one in the alley near the schoolhouse. It cast a silver light over the field, but the entrance of the building, recessed, was deep in shadow.

Ned was still talking to Victoria. He leaned close to her, took her by the hand, pulled her toward him. She did not resist or draw away as she did with the other boys. David's face burned. He could imagine vividly her quick smile, her large, slow-moving eyes, her ringing laughter, the sweet smell of soap on her body, the electric atmosphere about her, the impression of delicacy yet strength that her shape conveyed.

He could also imagine her sensing Ned's confident grin, his powerful chest, his deep vibrant voice, his pungent sweat.

They stood close together, their bodies touching. David's whole body was on fire. He would go down there, he would join them. He would make believe he was passing by and would stop and talk with them. But something kept him rooted there, like a spectator at a play who identifies himself with the actors and is involved in the action, but who can in no way influence it. Part of himself was Victoria and part of himself was Ned, with another self watching himself the actor, and a third self watching himself the observer.

Eva squealed. Willie George was unbuttoning her blouse. She shook her head and pulled away. He grabbed her arm and dragged her toward the doorway. She leaned back resisting and shrieking but her shrieks dissolved in giggles and she let herself be dragged along. They disappeared in the shadows.

Now Victoria and Ned turned. They too strolled toward the doorway. Ned's arm was around her waist. Victoria's arm was over Ned's shoulder. David could imagine under Victoria's fingers the sleekness of the rayon shirt, the hardness of Ned's swelling muscles. He could feel under Ned's fingers the narrowness of her waist, the ridges of her ribs, and, as his hand moved upward, the softness of her breast.

They were on the steps of the building. Ned pulled Victoria closer to him. She did not resist. They moved together into the shadows. David was trembling. He hated Ned. He hated Victoria. He would fight Ned. He would punch him to ribbons. Victoria, Victoria, why have you done this to me? Why have you betrayed me? You are no good. You are cheap, easy. No, why blame Victoria? You are a fool. How did you know she liked you? What made you think she was yours? How can you compete against Ned? What do you have to offer?

The book of poetry which he had been clutching slipped from his hand. He picked up the book. Through the window came a peal of laughter from Victoria. He flung the book down on the blanket with a sob. It was black dark now, too dark to read.

[1954]

WARS: AT HOME AND ABROAD

Memorial Wreath

*(It is a little-known fact that 200,000 Negroes fought
for freedom in the Union Army during the Civil War.)*

In this green month when resurrected flowers,
Like laughing children ignorant of death,
Brighten the couch of those who wake no more,
Love and remembrance blossom in our hearts
For you who bore the extreme sharp pang for us,
And bought our freedom with your lives.

                                      And now,
Honoring your memory, with love we bring
These fiery roses, white-hot cotton flowers
And violets bluer than cool northern skies
You dreamed of stooped in burning prison fields
When liberty was only a faint north star,
Not a bright flower planted by your hands
Reaching up hardy nourished with your blood.

Fit gravefellows you are for Douglass, Brown,
Turner and Truth and Tubman . . . . whose rapt eyes
Fashioned a new world in this wilderness.

American earth is richer for your bones:
Our hearts beat prouder for the blood we inherit.

[1942]

The Southern Road

There the black river, boundary to hell,
And here the iron bridge, the ancient car,
And grim conductor, who with surly yell
Forbids white soldiers where the black ones are.
And I re-live the enforced avatar
Of shuddering journey to a strange abode
Made by my sires before another war;
And I set forth upon the southern road.

To a land where shadowed songs like flowers swell
And where the earth is scarlet as a scar
Friezed by the bleeding lash that fell (O fell!)
Upon my fathers' flesh. O far, far, far
And deep my blood has drenched it. None can bar
My birthright to the loveliness bestowed
Upon this country haughty as a star.
And I set forth upon the southern road.

This darkness and these mountains loom a spell
Of peak-roofed town where yearning steeples soar
And the holy holy chanting of a bell
Shakes human incense on the throbbing air
Where bonfires blaze and quivering bodies char.
Whose is the hair that crisped, and fiercely glowed?
I know it; and my entrails melt like tar
And I set forth upon the southern road.

O fertile hillsides where my fathers are,
And whence my griefs like troubled streams have flowed,
Love you I must, though they may sweep me far.
And I set forth upon the southern road.

[1943]

Legacy: My South

What desperate nightmare rapts me to this land
Lit by a bloody moon, red on the hills,
Red in the valleys? Why am I compelled
To tread again where buried men have trod,
To shed my tears where blood and tears have flowed?
Compulsion of the blood and of the moon
Transports me. I was molded from this clay.
My blood must ransom all the blood shed here,
My tears redeem the tears. Cripples and monsters
Are here. My flesh must make them whole and hale.
I am the sacrifice.
                                    See where the halt
Attempt again and again to cross a line
Their minds have drawn, but fear snatches them back
Though health and joy wait on the other side.
And there another locks himself in a room
And throws away the key. A ragged scarecrow
Cackles an antique lay, and cries himself
Lord of the world. A naked plowman falls
Famished upon the plow, and overhead
A lean bird circles

[1943]

71

Games

The Battle of Waterloo was won on the playing fields of Eton.

—The Duke of Wellington

Not gunmen with his gat nor cop with billy
nor redskin with his ax and whoop could scare
wild kids who shouted in the windy air
of wide and weedy lots——Tom Jack and Willie
ran in their fathers' footsteps and when shrilly
their gats would gash them in their mock of men
they'd never fall but quick they'd rise again

But now, they are transported, willy-nilly,
To play a graver and a ghastlier game
On grander stage, in sea, on land, in air,
And kill where ever there are living men.
Oh, may the play which once they practiced there
Preserve them whole, and shelter them from shame,
Where, fallen once, they may not rise again.

[1942]

Rx

Love's a disease that's difficult to cure;
but purgatives of tears may have some power,
with regimen of loneliness, denial,
deceitfulness and falsehood and betrayal.
Injections of contempt may hasten health,
or daily immersions in a bath of filth.

And yet this maddening malady may linger
in spite of being cauterized with anger.
Even disillusion's sulfanilamide
against this sickness may give little aid.
So the remedy that proves the surest at last
is mould in the mouth and worms within the breast.

[1943]

Jailhouse Blues

I wish I was lyin
wrapped in my woman's arms.
O I wish I was lyin
safe in my woman's arms.
Then I wouldn't study to
do no one no harm.

I can get all the whisky
and gin that I can drink,
best Canadian whisky
and gin that I can drink.
I pour it down faster
than water runs down the sink.

I got a big radio
that plays ten records straight,
a fine big radio
plays ten records straight,
and a wide soft bed for
me and my lovin mate.

I got three women
to love me day and night,
black, brown and yellow
to love me day and night.
When I leave this jailhouse,
I'm sure gonna treat 'em right.

[1942]

74

The Apparition

To my sleep at night there comes a constant guest.
His eyes, deeper than any woman's eyes
that ever burned in mine, destroy my rest.
His voice, knifing and vibrant as the cries
of lovers at the summit of delight,
calls out my name with more than lovers' passion,
while his pale hands, that drip blood in the night,
reach to embrace me in forgiving fashion.

[1942]

Spring before a War

Spring came early that year.
Early the snow melted and crocuses took over
And in dooryard gardens blossomed the flower of the slain Greek boy.
Before the spring retired came roses
And orange lilies and great blanched spheres of peonies.
Days were warm and bright and fields promised incredible harvests,
And in meadows fresh and unscarred
With waists encircled and flanks touching
Strolled the dead boys
And the widowed girls.

[1944]

Helmeted Boy

Your forehead capped with steel
Is smoother than a coin
With profile of a boy who fell
At Marathon.

[1944–45]

Football Season

Now in the evenings rose and cool,
Tall above shadowed emerald grass,
With passion never given to school
Boys linger late to kick and pass.

Beneath their feet the green blades yield,
And seem, by some grave twilight change,
Familiar gridiron, lot, or field,
       And not the rifle range.

[1948]

Pacific Epitaphs

Rabaul
In far-off Rabaul
I died for democracy.
Better I fell
In Mississippi.

New Georgia
I loved to talk of home.
Now I lie silent here.

Treasury Islands
I mastered the cards,
The dice obeyed me.
But I could not palm
The number on the bullet.

Palawan
Always the peacemaker,
I stepped between
One buddy armed with an automatic
And another with a submachine gun.

Espiritu Santu
I hated guns,
Was a poor marksman,
But struck one target.

Iwo Jima
Like oil of Texas
My blood gushed here.

Bismarck Sea
Under the tossing foam
This boy who loved to roam
Makes his eternal home.

Tarawa
Tell them this beach
Holds part of Brooklyn.

Halmaherra
Laughing I left the earth.
Flaming returned.

New Guinea
A mosquito's tiny tongue
Told me a bedtime story.

Luzon
Splendid against the night
The searchlights, the tracers' arcs,
And the red flare of bombs
Filling the eye,
And the brain.

Coral Sea
In fluid element
The airman lies.

Bougainville
A spent bullet
Entered the abdominal cavity
At an angle of thirty-five degrees,
Penetrated the *pars pylorica,*
Was deflected by the *sternum,*
Pierced the *auricular dextral,*
And severed my medical career.

Vella Vella
The rope hugged tighter
Than the girl I raped.

Leyte
By twenty bolos hacked and beat,
He was a tender cut of meat.

Guadalcanal
Your letter.
These medals.
This grave.

Borneo
Kilroy
Is
Here.

[1944–45]

The Ascent

Into the air like dandelion seed
Or like the spiral of lark into the light
Or fountain into sun. All former sight
From hill or mountain was a mere hint of this.
We gain a new dimension. What had been
Our prison, where we crawled and clung like ants,
We spurn, and vision lying far beneath us.

O naked shape of earth! What green mammelles,
Arteries of gold and silver, turquoise flanks,
Plush jungles now are patterned! As we bank,
The earth tilts; we are level and aloof,
And it spins on and on among the stars.
We poise in air, hang motionless, and see
The planet turns with slow grace of a dancer.

[1948]

Coral Atoll

No wedding ring of doges, this white cirque that lies
dazzling, immaculate, upon the blue
of wide Pacific. High the airman sees
small ships crawl past it, and the surf exclaim
upon that O in foam less shining white.

No spiny island hurled out of the deep
by birthpangs of an earthquake is this round,
or green plateau that's sentient with warm life.
Things without thought, unvisioned and undreamed,
through mute numb years under the swaying tides
have died into a perfect form that sings.

[1944]

Wait For Me (Zhdi Myenya)

(Translated from the Russian of K. M. Simonov)

Wait for me, and I'll return.
Only surely wait.
Wait, when yellow autumn rains
Bring on long regret.
Wait, when snow whirls in the air,
Wait, when there is sun,
Wait, when others have forgot
And their waiting's done.
Wait, when letters come no more
From the faroff lines,
Wait, when he who also waits
Wearies and repines.

Wait for me, and I'll return.
Wish no happy lot
To the one who knows by heart
"Time that you forgot."
Son and mother may believe
That I am no more,
Friends may give me up and grieve,
And may sit before
The fire, drinking bitter wine
To my memory.
Wait. And with them gathered there
Do not drink to me.

Wait for me, and I'll return
Spite of all mishap.
Let the one who did not wait
Say, "A lucky chap."
Not remembering how when I
Struggled under fire
By your waiting for your own
You won your desire.

Only you and I will know
How I struggled through—
Simply, you knew how to wait
As no other knew.

[1951]

My Native Land (Rodina)

(Translated from the Russian of K. M. Simonov)

Touching three mighty and unending seas,
She lies, invincible, without a peer,
Spreading her cities and her distances
Over the black meridians of the sphere.

But in the moment when the last grenade
Lies ready to explode within your palm,
And all the things which on your heart have weighed
Must be remembered in that instant's calm,

Then you do not remember the wide land
Which you traversed and which you came to know,
But you remember what you understand
The best, your childhood home of long ago:

A piece of earth where three white birches grow,
A road that stretches to the forest floor,
A river with a ferry creaking slow,
A leaning willow and a sandy shore.

For here we had the luck to have our birth,
Here, all our lives, till death, we have possessed
A precious handful of the simple earth,
To be for us a sign of all the rest.

Yes, one can live through heat, through frost, through storm,
Yes, one can starve and freeze, can go to death,
But those three birches on a little farm
Can not be yielded while a man has breath.

[1951]

THE CIVIL RIGHTS ERA

Toward Mount Olympus

Ubi Sunt and Hic Sum

Thief, drunkard, brawler, it was the lot of François Villon, fifteenth century French poet, to write one of the loveliest evocations of the *Ubi sunt* (*Where are they?*) theme in all poetry. In the Middle Ages, with their pre-occupation with death, this theme was especially frequent, and Wyndham Lewis has called Villon's "Ballade of Dead Ladies" "one of the master songs of the world, with . . . the exquisite ache of its music, caressing and soothing to dreams, and its lovely refrain." It has recently been translated again by Richard Wilbur and by Galway Kinnell, but the most familiar version is by Dante Gabriel Rosetti.

> Tell me now in what hidden way is
> Lady Flora the lovely Roman?
> Where's Hipparchia, and where is Thais,
> Neither of them the fairer woman?
> Where is Echo, beheld of no man,
> Only heard on river and mere—
> She whose beauty was more than human? . . .
> But where are the snows of yester-year?

This poem was imitated by countless poets, until their imitations became a lifeless formula of dead princesses, kings, queens and anyone or anything else about whom or which one could ask, *"Ubi sunt?"*

Recently, however, the *Ubi sunt* theme was restored to vigorous life by a modern poet, Melvin B. Tolson, in *Harlem Gallery,* where he infuses color and gusto into the old theme.

> Where, oh, where is Bessie Smith
>   with her heart as big as the blues of truth?
> Where, oh, where is Mister Jelly Roll
>   with his Cadillac and diamond tooth?
> Where, oh, where is Papa Handy
>   with his blue notes a-dragging from bar to bar?
> Where, oh, where is bulletproof Leadbelly
>   with his tall tales and 12-string guitar?

Just as the *Ubi sunt* theme was prevalent in the Middle Ages with their concern for mortality; another theme, which I may call the *Hic sum,* or *Here I am,* theme, occurs again and again in American Negro poetry. Oppressed, ignored and deprecated, the Negro seeks identity and pride not by regretting or mourning past glories but by bringing them back to the present and identifying them with himself. Whether or not the poet is conscious of this theme and this tradition, it is an understandable psychological reaction to a social situation. One of the first and best-known poems with the *Hic sum* theme is Langston Hughes's "The Negro Speaks of Rivers," in which the Negro invests himself with the dignity and depth of ancient rivers.

I bathed in the Euphrates when dawns were young.
I built my hut near the Congo and it lulled me to sleep.
    I looked upon the Nile and raised the pyramids above it . . .

My soul has grown deep like the rivers.

Younger Negro poets have followed in his *Hic sum* tradition. There is Harold Lawrence's "Black Madonna" (*Negro Digest,* June 1962).

You were beautiful when
Your apparition formed
From Tanga mud and Rift;
Rocks of Rhodesia, Kush Ethiopia,
Sahara sands and Maya mounds,
And Grottes des Enfants,
Preserved your image.

Seventeen-year-old Gloria Davis writes, in "To Egypt," in Rosey Pool's new Dutch-English anthology, *Ik Ben de Nieuwe Neger,*

Tell them that my fathers, the pharaohs
were black. Let them know
Hannibal was my brother,
and that the temples soothed in blackness
were the toys of a foolish girl.

As long as the poets working this tradition bring to it something new-minted and unique to themselves, it will not become a mere formula, like the imitations of Villon. Birth, love, death are recurrent themes of poetry. But the other day I was thumbing through old numbers of the *Crisis* and found a poem using the *His sum* theme that was full of clichés. The poet called himself Crispus Attucks and Harriet Tubman and all the other stock figures, clothed in stock language, of Negro History Week.

The theme of *Hic sum* with its search for identity and pride need not be confined to Negro poets. We find it in the poem "Hebrews," by Samuel Oppenheim.

> I come of a mighty race . . . I come of a very mighty race . . .
> Adam was a mighty man, and Noah a captain of the moving waters,
> Moses was a stern and splendid king, yea, so was Moses.

We discover the *Hic sum* theme even in the work of the jaunty, optimistic white American Walt Whitman. But he inverts the material; instead of identifying the past with himself he rejects it and claims the present.

> Come Muse migrate from Greece and Ionia,
> Cross out please those immensely overpaid accounts,
> That matter of Troy and Achilles' wrath, and Aeneas',
> Odysseus' wanderings . . .
> For know a better, fresher, busier sphere, a wide,
> untried domain awaits, demands you.

When black American poets can do this, it will be a sign of profound changes in America.

[1965]

White Poet, Black Critic

In the attitude of a struggling poet who became famous toward a critic and anthologist who fostered poetry lies a lesson for young Negro intellectuals.

When Robert Frost was on his tour of Russia, after an exhausting visit to a Russian school he came back to the reserved section of his hotel dining room. Catching sight of a table of Arabians and a table of Chinese, he turned around and went back to his room, and ate there. "That's a bad prejudice of mine, isn't it?" he said.

This incident, reported by Franklin D. Reeve in *Robert Frost in Russia,* reveals an aspect of Frost which is different from the public image of the genial, philosophical sage of American poetry. Frost's letters, in the recent books *The Letters of Robert Frost to Louis Untermeyer* and *Selected Letters of Robert Frost,* also give views of a different facet of his personality.

Some of the letters reveal the Frost familiar to the public. He talks brilliantly of poetry. He shows a delight in words characteristic of a poet. The letters are full of puns and plays on words. The letters also disclose what is not so well known to the public, and round out and humanize the picture of the man. There was tragedy in his family life. He was often melancholy and without confidence in his poetry. He was suspicious, jealous of his fame, and shrewd in furthering his poetic career.

One of his plays on words was on the name of the Negro poet and critic, William Stanley Braithwaite. He wrote, "I'm not very angry with you for what you did to Breathweight. Only I wonder if he's worth all your pains. Perhaps he is. We were taught that we must try not to look down on anyone."

The man whom he called "Breathweight" was influential in the renaissance of American poetry in the early decades of the 1900s. As poetry critic of the *Boston Transcript,* he helped to bring the new poetry to the attention of the public by weekly articles, by full-scale book reviews, and by an annual summing up of the year's work in the field. With his *Anthology of Magazine Verse for 1913,* he was the first to publish a yearly anthology of verse in the United States.

The series continued until 1929, with a final volume for 1958 containing the best poems of that year and a selection of the best poems in the seventeen previous volumes. This series helped the reputations of poets, and increased the reading of poetry. Many poets and poems that later became famous were chosen, and poets were proud and excited to be included. Braithwaite also suggested to publishers the idea of yearly anthologies of short stories and of plays, two series which are still in existence today.

Claude McKay quotes a Negro historian on Braithwaite: "The most remarkable writer of Negro blood since Dunbar is William Stanley Braithwaite, who as a writer is not a Negro. . . . Mr. Braithwaite has by his literary production and criticism . . . his poems, his annual publication, *The Anthology of Magazine Verse,* demonstrated that the Negro intellect is capable of the same achievements as that of the whites."

When Claude McKay was coming into notice, he sent some poems to Braithwaite, who wrote to him that his poems were good, but that except for two of them any reader could tell that the author was a Negro. He advised McKay, because of the overwhelming prejudice against anything Negro, to write and send to the magazine only such poems as did not reveal his race. McKay did not take Braithwaite's advice. His own expression was too subjective and personal for him to write without conviction, and anyone who read him could tell that he came from a tropical country and was black.

In her memoirs, *Golden Friends I Had,* poet Margaret Widdemer tells of a party given in honor of Braithwaite. Notable poets and literary persons were there, but no Negroes. She says that she felt too much effusion in the praises given him, a sense of strain because of his color.

It was in the period of Braithwaite's achievement and influence that Frost first met him. He called on the critic in Boston. In his correspondence he shrewdly fed Braithwaite facts about himself which could be used in an article. Later he invited Braithwaite to visit him: "Would you come up about now? . . . Don't you think we could kill a week walking and talking?"

In 1915 Braithwaite selected some of Frost's poems for his anthology. Frost wrote, "I shall be honored if you will use the poems in your book, honored enough if you will use two, honored beyond dreams if you will use three." Braithwaite used "Birches" and "The Road Not Taken."

Frost wrote about the book: "I haven't read Braithwaite's g. d. book—I got one of the children to read it for me and tell me about it. All that saved the fat obstacle from the worst fate that overtakes paper was your name and mine on the flyleaf."

In a letter written as if coming from someone else to himself, Frost said: "Love is a kickshaw and dalliance naught, but give you a field like poetry that calls to the pulling of wires and the manipulation of ropes, to the climbing of every black reviewer's back stairs for preferment, and you [Frost] are there with a suitcase in both hands."

Thus, in spite of Braithwaite's fostering of American poetry, his promotion of Frost, and his determination to avoid anything that smacks of Negro, he is referred to as polluting the letter so that Frost breaks off and starts over on a fresh sheet.

Young Negro writers, who are pondering the question of identity, can learn from Braithwaite's experience.

[1965]

The Cut Throat

"One morning when this wretched creature was under my hands, I could resist the temptation no longer. With a quick, deft motion, I drew the razor across his throat."

Do you ever wonder what your barber is thinking, when he cuts your hair or shaves you? Besides being artists of a sort, we barbers are men of a thousand personalities, talkative when you feel like talking, respectful when you express an opinion, silent when you want to be quiet. We meet people of all types, and talk to infants and octogenarians, beggars and bankers, cops and criminals. But do you know what we are really like, underneath our mask of politeness?

While you relax in the soft chair, soothed with our hypnotic hands and the suave smell of balms and oils, you unwittingly confess things to us and expose the secret nooks and crannies of your souls. We know what goes on in your mind, but do you know what goes on in ours, as you lie helpless under our hands wielding the razor?

There was a man I had shaved for years. I began shaving him when the first soft down appeared upon his cheeks, and his skin was healthy and glowing. After I had shaved him, he would smile into the mirror and exclaim, "What a shave! What a barber you are!"

I would have a thrill of pride at a work of art well done. I shaved him the day he appeared in his best suit to be married, and the morning he came in disheveled after being up all night when his first child was born. I enjoyed watching him mature, and take on the responsibilities of a job, a wife, a family.

But somewhere along the road he began to falter. His responsibilities were more than he was willing or able to bear. He failed in his duties. Then he flouted them.

His hopes flickered out. He became bitter and quarrelsome. His friends avoided him. His wife left him, and took the children with her. He was burdened with debts.

He began to drink. His firm cheeks became flabby. Often, after he had spent a wild night, I would work over his strained face and look with regret into his bleary eyes.

I had liked him at first, but now I began to dislike him. He became repulsive to my touch. I wished that I didn't have to shave him, but it was a necessary job, as he insisted on putting up a front to the world and having his daily shave.

I tried to avoid shaving him, but he would always be there, demanding his daily rite from me alone, as if he were ashamed to have another barber touch him.

The shaves I gave him now were not so close and clean as they had been, but he would only glare into the mirror with a spiteful word and come back for another shave the next morning.

Sometimes he would not even care how he looked, but would stagger into the street without even inspecting my botched job.

Gradually I began to hate him. I began scheming of little ways to hurt or disfigure him. A slip of the razor here, a little nick there where it would be the most conspicuous.

He would swear when I cut him, or frown into the mirror and snarl, "What a butcher you turned out to be!" But still he demanded his daily shave, his badge of respectability to flash on the world.

At last I began to loathe him. It was then that I felt the temptation. Often, as I scraped the keen steel over his chin, I reflected that a little slip, a little pressure of the wrist, would cut his throat, and end his miserable existence. As I looked into his puffed features, I imagined how they would look with a wide red gash in his throat.

But I thought, "Who am I to take a life? Only God has the right to take a human life."

I wondered why I hated him so much. God, how I hated him. I hated everything about him. I hated him more than my worst enemy. I knew that possibly there were excuses for his degradation, but I hated him anyway.

And the temptation to kill him remained, persisted. I thought about it all day, and dreamed of it at night. The vision of his red cut throat became my fetish.

I could hardly wait for the morning hour when I would shave him and feel his throat under my fingers, his throat where, like an artist, I would carve my masterpiece.

One morning when this wretched creature was under my hands, I could resist the temptation no longer. With a quick, deft motion, I drew the razor across his throat. Some last-fraction-of-a-second feeling of pity, or of fear, perhaps, made me lighten the stroke. The wound was wide, but not deep, and did not prove fatal.

For the doctors tell me I will live.

[1951, 1964]

Shoe Shine Boy

The young one understood that, behind the old man's words and actions, was a way of life—a way of winning through against heavy odds.

Almost at the same instant, an Army sergeant and a young Negro entered the Men's room and walked toward the shoe shine stand just beyond the door. The sergeant was a step ahead, and as he climbed up to the chair the youth turned aside and began to wash and shave in one of the wash bowls at the end of the room.

"That's a lot of fruit salad you got on your chest, sir," the Negro attendant said.

"Yeah. I won most of these ribbons in Korea. And I got the rest in Viet Nam. Seems like I been killing yellow-bellies all my life."

"I bet you pizen to 'em, sir. You come home 'cause you tired of killing 'em?"

"Yeah. I'm gonna train our boys how to kill them slant-eyed bastards. Where's the other boy that was here last time I came through?"

"I'm the regular man here. He was just a substitute. I been working here thirty years. I really got rhythm."

He started brushing the sergeant's shoes, marking a subtle, syncopated rhythm that had the steady, onrushing beat of a steam locomotive. A man in shirt sleeves entered the room and stood nearby, watching.

The sergeant said, "You sure you been working here thirty years? You don't look that old to me. You ain't got a wrinkle on your face."

"Oh, yes, sir, thirty years at least."

"Take off your cap, Alexander, and let him see your hair," the bystander said.

Alexander shook his head. "No, sir. I don't take off my cap for nobody."

"Come on, boy, take off your cap," the sergeant wheedled. "Let's see what you got on that dome."

The bystander snatched off his cap. His head was bald, except for fringes of hair over his ears.

"Yeah, bald as a eight ball. I guess you are that old, but you sure don't look it."

"Don't you think I know how old I am?"

"Now, listen, boy. Don't get upset."

"No, sir. I was just funning. No fool, no fun. I wouldn't 've said that if I didn't like you. I just wanted to see how good your heart was."

The attendant changed from brushes to the polishing cloth. He developed a rhythm like the click of train wheels, punctuating it with staccato snaps of the cloth. He bent over the shoes, a virtuoso of rhythm. Rhythm possessed his whole body. He rocked from side to side. His buttocks began to wag to and fro in the intensity of his rhythm.

As if on cue, the bystander goosed him. He leaped into the air and burst into a frantic dance, but he still kept his rhythm, his feet drumming the floor in a wild beat, his eyes bugging.

"Oh, don't do that! Don't do that! I'm *sensitive!*"

The soldier rocked with laughter. The attendant resumed shining his shoes, but kept glancing fearfully over his shoulder until the shirt-sleeved man sauntered out.

He gave the cloth a final snap. "All done, sir," he said.

The soldier stepped down, smiled at the reflection in his shoes, dug in his pocket, and gave him a handful of silver.

"Oh, thank you! Thank you, sir!"

He followed the soldier to the door.

"Goodbye, sir! Have a nice trip, sir! God bless you, sir!"

The young Negro who had been shaving came and sat in the chair. The attendant glanced at his cracked, muddy shoes.

"I don't think I can do much with these."

"Do the best you can. I know they're full of mud."

"What kind of mud you got there? Mississippi mud?"

"Yeah. Mississippi mud."

"Mississippi your home?"

"No. Cleveland."

"What was you doing down there?"

"Working."

"Find plenty work down there?"

"Yeah. Plenty."

"What kind of work was you doing?"

"I was trying to get people to register to vote."

"Oh. You one of them—freedom fighters?"

"Yeah. I guess you could call it that."

"Those crackers, they pretty mean."

"Yeah. Pretty mean."

"What you doing up here? Going home?"

"Yeah. To Cleveland. They said I needed a rest."

"You gonna stay in Cleveland?"

"No, I'm gong back to Mississippi as soon as I can. Soon as I raise some money."

"You know, the way I was talking to that soldier—sometimes you gotta act a certain way even if you don't feel like that inside."

"I know what you mean."

"You make 'em feel like a big shot, they tip you like a big shot."

"Yeah. I've noticed that."

"I ain't got no education. This is all I know how to do. Been working here thirty years. Raised a daughter and put her through high school."

"I know how it is."

The attendant snapped his cloth and stepped back.

"There. They look a hundred per cent better."

The young man stepped down and reached into his pocket.

"No. No charge. It's for the movement."

"Thank you, brother." He reached for his canvas bag.

The attendant followed him to the door.

"Goodbye, sir! Have a nice trip, sir!" he checked himself.

"*God bless you,*" he whispered.

[1962]

Incident on a Bus

He was just a shabby little Negro, and while he may have been dirty, it would never have occurred to anyone that he also was dangerous.

After the demonstrations, the arrests, the trials and the negotiations, the city administration reluctantly agreed to desegregate the buses. But the Ku Klux Klan threatened to picket—and the Citizens Group to boycott—the buses, and Jones's editor told him to ride on and get the story.

Jones entered a bus and took a seat at the back, so as to have a good view of all the passengers. The bus was passing through a Negro area which encircled the downtown district. Almost half the passengers were Negroes. There was no tension, but an air of expectancy, in the bus.

Jones realized that it was up to the Negroes to integrate the bus. The whites were not going to sit in the back, which bore the stigma of being the worst place. Strange, he thought, in a train or an airplane the Jim Crow place was the front, while in a bus it was the back.

The Negroes were proceeding to integrate the bus. A couple got on and sat down directly behind the driver, and there were others scattered through the front and the middle. They avoided sitting next to whites. They sat next to each other or took vacant seats.

As the bus passed through Skid Row, a little nondescript Negro man got on. He was the sort you'd see and never remember. He wore nondescript clothes and had nondescript features which you'd forget as soon as you saw them.

He peered around for a seat, saw one next to an elderly white man, and sat down in it. The man had been hogging his seat, sitting almost in the middle, perhaps to discourage any Negro from sitting next to him, and the new passenger had to sit half in the aisle. To get more room, he slid closer to the old man. He did not move over, but turned around and stared angrily at the Negro. The Negro kept on pushing and leaned close against him. He glared at the little man with the most virulent hate in his thin face and pale blue eyes that Jones had ever seen. Even Jones was seared with the malignancy of it. Hell, he thought, that look is enough to melt a brass monkey. Will that little fellow have enough guts to keep on?

Apparently he did, for he kept on pushing vigorously and pressing close to the occupant. All at once the old man yielded and jerked sideways and pressed stiffly against the window, his face jammed against the glass as if he were trying to move as far as possible from the hated presence of the Negro.

Well, that little fellow had the nerve not to give up, Jones thought, even though the old man is hating his guts for sitting next to him. Hurrah for you, little man.

But the little man seemed not to enjoy his victory. He squirmed uncomfortably on the seat. He peered around furtively, and after a couple of stops he scampered to the door and skipped off the bus, a dun-colored little mouse, so timid and insignificant looking that you only half glanced at him and forgot him as soon as you saw him.

The old man remained in the same position, jammed against the side of the bus with his face pressed against the pane.

He must have asked the driver to call his stop, for two or three blocks farther on the driver called a street loudly and looked in his mirror at the man. When he did not get up, the driver walked back to him and said, "Here's your stop."

He did not answer and the driver touched his shoulder. Bending over him, he touched him again, then jerked back his hand and stared at it. It was red with blood.

"Jesus Christ!" he said. "The man is dead."

[1964–65]

Booker T. and W. E. B.

(Booker T. Washington and W. E. B. Du Bois)

"It seems to me," said Booker T.,
"It shows a mighty lot of cheek
To study chemistry and Greek
When Mister Charlie needs a hand
To hoe the cotton on his land,
And when Miss Ann looks for a cook,
Why stick your nose inside a book?"

"I don't agree," said W. E. B.
"If I should have the drive to seek
Knowledge of chemistry or Greek,
I'll do it. Charles and Miss can look
Another place for hand or cook.
Some men rejoice in skill of hand,
And some in cultivating land,
But there are others who maintain
The right to cultivate the brain."

"It seems to me," said Booker T.,
"That all you folks have missed the boat
Who shout about the right to vote,
And spend vain days and sleepless nights
In uproar over civil rights.
Just keep your mouths shut, do not grouse,
But work, and save, and buy a house."

"I don't agree," said W. E. B.,
"For what can property avail
If dignity and justice fail?
Unless you help to make the laws,
They'll steal your house with trumped-up clause.
A rope's as tight, a fire as hot,
No matter how much cash you've got.
Speak soft, and try your little plan,

But as for me, I'll be a man."

"It seems to me," said Booker T.—

"I don't agree,"
Said W. E. B.

[1952]

Ballad of Birmingham

"Mother dear, may I go downtown
instead of out to play,
and march the streets of Birmingham
in a freedom march today?"

"No, baby, no, you may not go,
for the dogs are fierce and wild,
and clubs and hoses, guns and jails
aren't good for a little child."

"But, mother, I won't be alone.
Other children will go with me,
and march the streets of Birmingham
to make our country free."

"No, baby, no, you may not go,
for I fear those guns will fire.
But you may go to church instead,
and sing in the children's choir."

She has combed and brushed her nightdark hair,
and bathed rose petal sweet,
and drawn white gloves on her small brown hands,
and white shoes on her feet.

The mother smiled to know her child
was in the sacred place,
but that smile was the last smile
to come upon her face.

For when she heard the explosion,
her eyes grew wet and wild.
She raced through the streets of Birmingham
calling for her child.

She clawed through bits of glass and brick,
then lifted out a shoe.
"O, here's the shoe my baby wore,
but, baby, where are you?"

[1963]

Dressed All in Pink

(November 22, 1963, the assassination of President John F. Kennedy)

It was a wet and cloudy day
when the prince took his last ride.
The prince rode with the governor,
and his princess rode beside.

"And would you like to ride inside
for shelter from the rain?"
"No, I'll ride outside, where I can wave
and speak to my friends again."

They ride among the cheering crowds,
the young prince and his mate.
The governor says, "See how they smile
and cheer you where they wait."

The prince rides with the governor,
his princess rides beside,
dressed all in pink as delicate
as roses of a bride.

Pink as a rose the princess rides,
but bullets from a gun
turn that pink to as deep a red
as red, red blood can run,

for she bends to where the prince lies still
and cradles his shattered head,
and there that pink so delicate
is stained a deep, deep red.

The prince rides with the governor,
the princess rides beside,
and her dress of pink so delicate
a deep, deep red is dyed.

[1964]

Hymn

Squat and ugly in your form,
but fierce as Moloch in your power,
accept our worship and our warm
dependence in this demon hour.

While problems of the world and state
knot up our minds with anguished choice,
yours is the power to extirpate
all cavil with volcanic voice.

And then no more of wrong or right,
or whose shrewd counsels we should keep.
One flash of sun-outshouting light,
and then the dark, forgetful sleep.

[1962]

Frederick Douglass and the Slave Breaker

I could have let him lash me
like a horse or a dog
to break my spirit.
Others never lifted a finger.
I would have been just one more.

But something in me said, "Fight.
If it's time to die, then die for *some*thing.
And take him with you."

So all day long we battled,
the man and the boy, sweating,
bruising, bleeding . . .

till at last the slave breaker said,
"Go home, boy. I done whupped you enough.
Reckon you done learned our lesson."

But I knew who it was that was whipped.
And the lesson I learned
I'll never forget.

[1972]

Interview

What's going on there? Why the wrestling match?
Let go that fellow. Bring him here to me.

You're rather rumpled from this roughing up,
But otherwise in right good shape. And so
You crossed the moat and climbed the barbed-wire fence,
Escaped the dogs and dodged the guards' revolvers
And got this close to me with just a necktie
Twisted out of place, a swollen lip,
And rumpled coat that even now you're brushing
Back into shape. And how? Who did you bribe,
Flatter, browbeat or blackmail to crash in?
But never mind. I'll find that out. And someone
Will smart for that. But what are you doing here?
Are you another crackpot come to shoot me
Or pester me with plans to save the world?
You're a reporter, want an interview?

Isn't your editor satisfied with the statements
My staff mailed out about the new Foundation?
All of the facts were there: the greatest sum
Ever devoted to philanthropy
Donated for research in education,
Science and medicine to make life better.
My brightest boys devised that press release,
Full of the hokum that pleases the public best.
But you want more? My own ideas and views?

Well, I'm an old man, and a sick one too,
Or so these pill-men say, and seldom talk
For public hearing. (My advisers tell me
My tongue's too sharp.) But since you've been rough-handled
And seem a bold-faced youngster much like me
When I was your age, I'll talk frankly to you,

And what you think the public can digest
You're free to write. The rest, use for yourself.

Some say the Fund's to cheat the state of taxes.
Others, more kind, insist it's just a way
To pay back mankind what I've robbed them of.
They're all mistaken. What I want, I take.
And what I take, I keep. Why give it back?
I never thought the world was made for me.
It has its own laws, rolls along as merry
As if I were not here, nor ever had been.
So why should I complain if my toe's crushed?

What I have done is to observe its ways,
And having learned them, use them to advantage.
Are men dishonest, petty, greedy, vain?
Why should I pule and murmur if they are?
I'll use their greed and vanity to my ends,
Not snivel, try to reform the world, and fail.
I've used the world for what it is, and gained
A many million. Now it is my whim
To try to change the world, and prove to those
Who could not take the world just as they found it
And therefore lack the power to change it at all
That one old, greedy, and predacious villain
Can do more good in the world than all of them
In all their years of whining and complaining.
And, what is more, they'll be my instruments.

So here's my story. Use it as you want to.
You needn't send a galley. I'll get your name
From the signed article. And remember it.

The Dilemma

My poems are not sufficiently obscure to please the critics.
—Ray Durem

I'd like to sing (but singing is naïve)
To express emotion freely and unveiled,
(But should I wear my heart upon my sleeve,
And as a lush Romantic be assailed?)
And sometimes I would like to make a plain
Unvarnished statement bare of metaphor,
(But to speak simply is to be inane;
A man of the world should never be a bore.)

And so I cultivate my irony,
And search strange books for the recondite allusion.
The time's confused, so I must also be,
and in the reader likewise plant confusion.
So, though no Shelley, I'm a gentleman,
And, if not Attic, Alexandrian.

[1956]

Poet

Patron of pawn shops,
Sloppily dressed,
Bearded, tieless, and shoeless,
Reading when you should be working,
Fingering a poem in your mind
When you should be figuring a profit,
Convert to outlandish religions,
Zen, Ba'hai and Atheism,
Consorter with Negroes and Jews
And other troublesome elements
Who are always disturbing the peace
About something or other,
Friend of revolutionaries
And foe of the established order,
When will you slough off
This preposterous posture
And behave like a normal
Solid responsible
White Anglo Saxon Protestant?

[1957]

Aphorisms

He who vilifies the Jew
next day will slander you.

He who calls his neighbor "nigger"
upon your turning back will snigger.

He who vaunts a Master Race
brings upon his line disgrace.

While he who calls a faith absurd
thrusts the spear into his Lord.

[1962]

The Intellectuals

The intellectuals talked.

They had to decide on principles.
Nothing should be done, nothing legislated
Till a rationale had been established.

The intellectuals talked.

Meanwhile the others,
Who believed in action,
And that they should be up and all the rest down,
Stormed the hall, shot the leaders and arrested the remainder,
Whom they later hanged.

[1963]

Straight Talk from a Patriot

If the gooks in Viet Nam refuse to see
The virtue of our great democracy,
We'll make them see it—if we have to bomb
Or burn the whole damn country with napalm.

[1968]

Daily News Report

We killed 250 men today.

We
    we *killed*
         we killed *two*
            we killed two *hundred*
               we killed two hundred *fifty*
                  we killed two hundred fifty *men*
today

Today
    were living
        two
            two *hundred*
              two hundred *fifty*
                two hundred fifty *men*
were living
    today

Now they are dead
    We killed them
        We *killed*
            KILLED
               KILLED
them
    today

[1968–69]

Blood Precious Blood

Blood
precious blood,
yours, Medgar,
yours, Malcolm,
yours, Martin,
flowing spreading sweeping
covering flooding drowning.

What can wash cleanse purify redeem this land
stained
with your blood,
your precious blood?

[November 12, 1968]
[December 7, 1980]

A Leader of the People

(For Roy Wilkins)

I give my life to my people.
Oppressed, poor, starving.
Pushed away, knocked down, trod upon.
They murder our men, rape our women,
starve our children of food and affection.
I will lead them to a better life,
to self-respect and independence.

Many will hate you for this.

I can bear hate for the love of my people.

They will rebuke you and scorn you.
They will laugh at you and deride you.
They will malign you and lie about you.
They will smear your name with filth.

I can bear scorn for the pride of my people.

They will bruise you with stones.
They will beat you with sticks.
They will pierce you with arrows.
At last they will hang you from a tree until you are dead.

I will suffer these pangs from my enemies to save my people.

It is not your enemies who will do these things to you,
but your people.

[1980]

Melvin B. Tolson

Portrait of a Poet as Raconteur

"I found him to be, as Langston Hughes has described him, a man who can talk to students, cotton-pickers and cowpunchers, a great talker—a very warm and human person."

I have not had many opportunities to talk to Great Men, and most of those occasions came to nothing. Either I would meet them as I was in a line of well-wishers and would be elbowed out of the way by the next person in line, or after they had dropped a few perfunctory commonplaces upon me they would be swept to tea or cocktails by Important People.

With M. B. Tolson, however, it was different. One night poet-sculptor Oliver LaGrone telephoned me that Tolson was in town and invited me to come and meet him. I found him to be, as Hughes has described him, a man who can talk to students, cotton-pickers and cowpunchers, a great talker—a very warm and human person.

With his bald head fringed by gray tufts over his ears and his seamed, smiling face, he looked like an old-fashioned preacher. When he settled back in his chair, took a cigar in his right hand and a glass in his left and remarked that tonight he would forget about Jim Crow and concentrate on Old Crow, we knew that we were in for a night of good talk. Inasmuch as many critics have hailed him as a great poet but none has mentioned his supremacy as a talker, I am going to enlarge on this aspect of his talent.

His style is expansive. This may come from his many years at Wiley and Langston as a college professor with a captive audience. Or it may spring from his natural tendency to expatiate. Both his prize-winning *Dark Symphony* and his *Libretto for the Republic of Liberia* are long poems, and his 173-page *Harlem Gallery* is only part one of a projected poem in four parts. He is not a poet given to short swallow flights of song. He never cuts through the barn when it is possible to stroll around it. But, during his walk around the barn, he dispenses treasures of observation, learning and humor culled from vast experience and reading.

An example of his indirect method, as well as his Socratic method of teaching by questioning, is his anecdote about a white Northern club woman who was distressed because a Southern member of her club asserted that Negroes steal chickens. Instead of denying this, Tolson asked, "Did you ever see movies of a southern mansion with a huge dining hall and chandeliers and a linen-covered table where old Colonel sat down to dinner with his family?"

"Yes," she answered.

"And, did you see a black butler in a white coat bringing in a platter of fried chicken balanced high in the air with one hand?"

"Yes."

"Well, black Sam served the chicken. And who cooked the chicken?"

"His wife, I guess."

"Yes, black Mandy sweated over the stove to cook the chicken. And who fed and watered and took care of the chicken?"

"His daughter, I suppose?"

"Yes, little Cindy raised that chicken. And who grew the corn and crops that fattened the chicken so the Colonel could eat it?"

"The butler's son?"

Yes, black Junior toiling in the fields raised the corn to fatten that chicken. But, who ate the chicken?"

By this time the clubwoman had begun to see the point and was smiling. "The Colonel, of course."

"Yes, the Colonel ate that chicken. But somewhere on that plantation was a black Patrick Henry who said, 'Give me liberty, or give me—chicken!' Now, did the colonel give him his liberty?"

"No," the woman answered with a smile.

Then as Tolson described with mock-Freudian symbols how the slave captured the hen by tickling its rump with a long pole, the woman shook with laughter, and, he says, she was never again disturbed by the southern woman's allegations that Negroes stole chickens.

Tolson could have answered her simply by saying that this was compensation for economic and social exploitation, but instead of using the abstract jargon of the sociologist he dramatized the situation with the invention and humor of the poet.

Another characteristic of his talk is his ability to adjust it to his audience. I heard him on two occasions, once when he was with a group of young poets and again when he was in a group of non-writers.

On the first occasion he acted as a catalyst, advising the poets to study and revise, demonstrating for those who thought knowledge of technique would destroy their spontaneity that it would make their work stronger, showing those who thought that they could not improve their first inspirations that they could make them better, telling those pressed for time to write that he worked after midnight in the company of cats and owls, admonishing them that poetry was performance and not propaganda.

He told many literary anecdotes. He said the critic V. F. Calverton praised him as having the potential of becoming the greatest Negro poet. Tolson was non-plused and said, "You flatter me."

Calverton replied, "Why in hell should I flatter *you*?"

Tolson said that at Breadloaf Writers' Conference Saul Bellow called him "subversive," because the young poets would bring beer and hamburgers to his cottage at night and would sit on the floor listening to his anecdotes until the small hours and would oversleep and miss their sessions the next day.

One of the poets who was present that night wrote, "I'll never forget Mr. Tolson's marvelous mind and simple humility and absolute integrity!"

Tolson related that after completing *Libretto for the Republic of Liberia* he asked Allen Tate to write a preface for it, and Tate replied that he wasn't interested in the propaganda of Negro poets. Tolson spent a year studying modern poetic techniques and rewriting the poem so that it said the same things in a different way and then sent it to Tate. Tate wrote a preface in which he said, "For the first time, it seems to me, a Negro poet has assimilated the full poetic language of his time."

If the first version of the poem still exists, it would be interesting to see it in a variorum edition with the re-written version, and to compare them.

Tolson is modest about his achievements. He admits that he began as a mediocre poet, but developed his art by learning and experimenting. He says that *Dark Symphony* is a good poem, but not a great one. At a lecture he read his poem "My Soul and I" and, after the applause had died down, startled the audience by saying, "That was a bad poem. You shouldn't have applauded." He proceeded to analyze the poem phrase by phrase and line by line, explaining where and how it was bad and how he had improved it by revision.

With the second, non-writing group, Tolson's talk was entirely different. He did not refer to poetry at all, except to remark that perhaps the reason he was unknown among his own people was that "when white people want to hide something from Negroes, they put it in a book or a magazine."

Since his host was a graduate of Wiley College, where Tolson had taught and had coached the debating team, he reminisced upon his experiences there. He told of taking the team to the University of Southern California and scouting the speech department, which was as large as all of Wiley College. When he got back, the team asked about their opponents and wanted to visit the campus. He told them, "They're not so much. We'll visit them after we win the debate, just to show them we're good sports." Little Wiley College won the debate.

Tolson has great gusto as a talker. The night I met him, LaGrone and I left early, as he was convalescing from a major operation. But we found out later that he had learned that James Farmer, one of his students, was in Detroit, and telephoning until he located him, he had gone out and spent the night in talk and had not returned to his sister's home until five o'clock the next morning.

At his home in Langston, Oklahoma, he formed a Zulu Club, like the Zulu Club Wits in *Harlem Gallery*, where men meet to discuss and exchange ideas. Chapters have been formed in various cities across the country. They are composed of men of all occupations, from professional men to laborers—anyone who is interested in reading, thinking and exchanging ideas.

In his conversation he hints of some day writing his autobiography, *The Life and Times of M. B. Tolson*.

Retired now from his position at Langston University, he occupies a newly created chair in humanities at Tuskegee Institute, with only one class to teach. It will be profitable if he can use his new-found leisure not only to complete *Harlem Gallery*, but also to write his memoirs, as they should be invaluable for the humor, the recollections of literary figures, and the record of the poetic development of this gifted poet and raconteur.

[1966]

POEMS ON MISCELLANEOUS SUBJECTS

Hail, Dionysos

Hail, Dionysos,
god of frenzy and release, of trance and visions,
hail to the manifestations of your might,
thanks for admitting me to your ritual.

Inspirer of divine speech:
  da da da da da da da da da;
releaser of subterranean energies:
  a man lies snoring on the sofa;
giver of fierce grace:
  a girl staggers among chairs, reels against the wall;
endower with new sensations and powers:
  a man vomits on the rug—an aromatic painting,
  and a girl, a lovely creature,
  wets her panties.

Hail, Dionysos,
god of frenzy and release, of trance and visions.

I see them recede,
handsome men, beautiful women,
brains clever and bright, spirits gay and daring,
see eyes turn glassy, tongues grow thick,
limbs tremble and shake,
caught in your divine power,
carried away on the stream of your might,
Dionysos.

Analysands

Sipping whiskey and gin,
they analyze their analysts and their treatment
in jargon like the debris in a magpie's gullet.
Each feeling, each phrase, each dream
is dissected with dialectic keener than a scalpel.
Like lactating women unbrassiering and comparing their breasts
or small boys measuring their penises,
they incise themselves,
draw out and display their entrails,
tear out their throbbing dripping hearts
and scrutinize each minute quivering,
till finally, full of whiskey and gin,
they drop asleep on sofa, chair or floor.

Winter Campus: Ann Arbor

April took flesh in clear September air
when one girl paused upon the colonnade,
turned, and for a heartbeat hovered there
while yellow elm leaves drifted past her hair.

Here, now, the same soft youngness is conveyed
as these bareheaded throngs stream to and fro
with footfalls noiseless in the sudden snow,
a hum like bees pulsating on and on
while treble voices tremble in the air
and rime with chiming of the carillon.

[1950–51]

Shape of the Invisible

At dawn
Upon the snow
The delicate imprint
Left by the sleeping body of
The wind.

[1942]

Nocturne

Light has laid down its chisel.
Only a staring, mutilated moon
crawls over the dim meadows of the mind
where my love lies irrevocably lost,
beyond the clasp of pity or desire.

In recollection's mists her face is blurred,
and she has left no spoor
except, perhaps, in caverns of a dream,
or in the insinuations of a willow.

[1963]

Augury for an Infant

(For Venita Sherron)

Venita, you have come to us.
What will you be?
Proud as Du Bois, humble as Booker T.?
A poet with the humor of Dunbar,
or with the fiery feelings of Antar?
Classic as Pushkin, romantic as Dumas?

There's so much wealth to mine,
so much to do.
Will you be a Carver, Banneker, or Drew,
or learn the lore of the Ethiopian queen?
Sing sweet as Marian or Leontyne?
Or be an artist, skilled, sophisticated
as those by whom the African bronzes were created?

In you, little babe, I see
Infinite possibility.

[1963]

Belle Isle

Joy and delight, joy and delight, like bells
Or bell-like flowers pealing in memory.

When leaves were the color of sun,
And the island floated toward winter,
You exclaimed at the freighters surging past,
And reached for words to express their masterful glide.
You laughed at the insolent motorboats
Hurling their foaming wake upon the shore,
Delighted in a blue-sailed vessel, and in the flowerhouse
You reveled in the bright-leaved plants,
Grew ecstatic at a firmament of bell-like flowers,
Reached on tiptoe to steal a blossom
And pinched a stem to grow "by love" you said.

You listened for the tinkle of the carousel
And mixed your laughter with its melody,
And food and drink and cigarets were part.

I, watching, thought: This is how poets are.
This is the inner principle of their art:
Joy and delight, joy and delight, poems
Conceived in joy, endowing the world and time
With joy and delight, joy and delight, for ever.

[1964]

Verse Forms

Free verse is a club.
If it batters long enough,
It may crush a breastplate.

A sonnet is an arrow.
Pointed and slim, it pierces
The slit in the armor.

[1980]

Poem, on a Nude, from the Ballet, to Debussy's *Prelude L'Après-Midi D'un Faune,* after Mallarmé's *L'Après-Midi D'un Faune*

Killing a Bug

That little black dot
Felt fear and panic
As it shot
Across the table
Not
Able
To linger
Before my finger
Smashed it.

Will I
Feel such fear and try
To hide and linger
When I chance to stray
To a place and day
Where some Eye
Will brush me
And a huge Finger
Crush me?

And will He
Be
As careless and uncaring
As I
In my
Smearing?

[1980]

LOVE POEMS

I Loved You Once (Ya Vas Lyubil)

(Translated from the Russian of Alexander Pushkin*)

I loved you once; love even yet, it may be,
within my soul has not quite died away.
But let that cause you no anxiety;
I would not give you pain in any way.
I loved you silently, and hopelessly,
with jealousy, timidity brought low,
I loved you so sincerely, tenderly
I pray to God some other love you so.

[1949]

* Alexander Pushkin was the Russian poet of African descent
who is credited for making the Russian language live again.

The Profile on the Pillow

After our fierce loving,
in the brief time we found to be together,
you lay in the half-light
exhausted, rich,
with your face turned sideways on the pillow,
and I traced the exquisite
line of your profile, dark against the white,
delicate and lovely as a child's.

Perhaps
you will cease to love me,
or we may be consumed in the holocaust,
but I keep, against the ice and the fire,
the memory of your profile on the pillow.

[1968 (THE YEAR OF THE FIRE AND THE WHIRLWIND)]

Good to Be in You

Good to be in you.
Good, too, to be near you.
To feel your shoulder touching mine
and know that all night we shall lie side by side,
and in the morning
you will wake me with your gentle movements about the room.

Good to be in you.
Good, too, to be with you.
To sit at table and look into your eyes
and see feelings, like wind over grass or water,
stir your sensitive face,
to exchange our families and our childhoods,
and know that our souls have kissed.

Thunderstorm

June.—Night.—Rain.——And thunder
of our hearts together.

Black Magic

Black girl black girl
lips as curved as cherries
full as grape bunches
sweet as blackberries

Black girl black girl
when you walk you are
magic as a rising bird
or a falling star

Black girl black girl
what's your spell to make
the heart in my breast
jump———stop———shake

[1969]

The Brightness Moved Us Softly

Light flowed between black branches and new snow
into the shaded room and touched your eyes.
Your slow lids made another soft sun rise
upon your face, and as that morning glow
spread in your cheeks and blushed upon your lips,
the brightness moved us softly to a kiss.

Love Poem

Love lover beloved loved one
lovely lovelier loveliest lovable love
love loveless lovelorn lovelone lovelack lacklove
unloved misloved disloved underloved subloved
lovingkindness lovingcare tenderlove dearlove
sweetlove kindlove heartlove soullove
lovelily lovingly lovedlily lovably
lovelook lovetouch lovespeech lovetalk
closelove tightlove nightlove dawnlove
morninglove freshlove lovecalls lovecries
love love love love love love love
relove overlove surlove superlove
everloving heavenlove soullove heartlove truelove
loveosity lovefeats lovefeast lovefest
loveniks lovadors lovathons longlove lastinglove
lovability lovingness reloved surloved superloved
loveliness lover beloved loved one love done
love you love you love you love you

Sanctuary

This is the time of the whirlwind and the fire.
This is the time of nation-death-and-birth.
And from the turbulence there is no shelter,
except within the circle of love's arms,
where for a moment, in that little space,
you may find peace and tenderness,
even in the center of the fiery winds.

So step into the circle of my arms
while we are hurled, with the other doomed spirits,
around and around in the fury of the whirlwind.

[1968]

Love Song

Until the shadows go,
And morning gilds the copse,
Beloved, be like a doe
Upon the mountain tops.

As softly as the snow
Upon the mountain drops,
Your love on me bestow
Until the shadows go
And morning gilds the copse.

Beloved, be like a doe,
Upon the mountain tops.

April Mood

This is the season when, in days of old,
Young knights would don again their dinted arms,
And, as in tales at great length we are told,
Would venture forth through forests fields and farms
To rescue damsels from magicians' charms
And saucy worms exhaling sultry flame,
And out of hard encounters, fierce alarms
Would win eternal glory and a dame.
So, though I am not quite on fire for fame,
And though few ogres live upon my street,
Beloved, can you hold me much to blame
If in this month so stirring and so sweet
     Something extraordinary I wish to do
     To prove my valor, and my love for you?

[1965]

Loss

Your leaving is like a severed arm.
It——hurts. I reach to touch it.
Nothing's——there.

[1973]

Green Apples

What can you do with a woman under thirty?
It's true she has a certain freshness, like a green apple,
but how raw, unformed, without the mellowness of maturity.

What can you talk about with a young woman?
That is, if she gives you a chance to talk,
as she talks and talks and talks about herself.
Her——self——is the most important object in the universe.
She lacks the experience of intimate, sensitive silences.

Why don't young women learn how to make love?
They attack with the subtlety of a bull,
and moan and sigh with the ardor of a puppy.
Panting, they pursue their own pleasure,
forgetting to please their partner, as an older woman does.

It's only just that young women get what they deserve.
A young man.

[1972]

Anniversary Words

You who have shared my scanty bread with me
and borne my carelessness and forgetfulness
with only occasional lack of tenderness,
who have long patiently endured by faculty
for genial neglect of practicality,
for forgetting the morning and the parting caress
and for leaving rooms in a great disorderliness
which when I entered were as neat as they could be,

despite the absent-mindedness of my ways
and the not seldom acerbity of your tone,
I sometimes catch a softness in your gaze
which tells me after all I am your own
and that you love me in no little way.
But I know it best by the things you never say.

DIALECTICS OF THE BLACK AESTHETIC

Black Power

The fact that CORE and SNCC have taken different roads from the NAACP, the Urban League, and SCLC does not lead me to believe that the civil rights movement as a whole is at a crossroads, where one road can lead to success and the other to disaster. The older organizations are continuing in the way they have always taken, using legal techniques, moral persuasion, non-violent demonstrations, and cooperation with whites.

There has been a tendency in the two younger organizations to develop grass-roots leadership and power, a tendency which is now coming to the fore. Instead of taking one road, the civil rights movement is taking two roads. In my opinion, this is a good thing, as the problem of racism cannot be solved by any panacea. It needs to be attacked on a variety of fronts, by whatever tactic is most effective in a given situation.

Our leaders have used too much energy fighting and criticizing each other. From the utterances of some of them, it would seem that other Negro leaders are greater enemies to the civil rights movement than white bigots. Every one has his favorite solution, strategy, and tactics, but that does not mean that other tactics and approaches are not effective and should not be used.

I would not consider the civil rights movement to be at a crossroads, because if direct political action fails, there is still the alternative of legal and persuasive techniques employed by the older organizations. If these methods prove ineffectual, there are the techniques of political and economic mobilization already adopted by the other two organizations.

I think we should beware of expecting perfection or Utopia. As President Kennedy said, life is hard, some men spend the war state-side and others are killed. I think we should constantly strive toward perfection but not be too disappointed if we do not achieve it.

In my opinion, Black Power means organizing black people so that they can have power commensurate with their numbers in their communities, states, and in the nation. This will mean that they may dominate some communities politically, will be a strong force in some states, and will wield power in the national government. This is similar to what other groups have done.

In the Detroit suburb of Hamtramck, for instance, the Poles regularly elect a Polish mayor, Polish state representatives and senators, and Polish representatives to Congress. The Irish have long dominated Boston, and recently we had an Irish Catholic President. We have Catholic power, Jewish power, Italian power, and Armenian power. Let there be Black Power too. Black people have long voted for whites to represent them; now whites should learn to vote for black representatives. It's the ability of the man which matters, not the color of his skin.

The adverse reaction of the white press to the phrase "Black Power" stems from two things, the whites' attitude toward blacks and their feelings about themselves. One of the things which incenses the black man toward the white is his absolute refusal to see the black man. To the white, he is invisible, not there. A white makes a movie or a television show about a hospital, say, where black interns, nurses, and orderlies are falling over each other, but the picture will be lily white. There may be a promotion coming up, but he never considers competent black workers for the position. To him the black man is invisible, he does not exist.

Or, he may indeed see the black man, but through the distortion of his own preconceptions and prejudice. Sixty years ago, if you mentioned black writers to a white bigot, he would say, "A nigger write a book? How can an ape write a book?" Today, at the term "Black Power," many whites have the same reaction; the only difference is that it is stated in more genteel language.

The second reason for the whites' reaction to the term "Black Power" is internal—their sense of guilt. When you have kidnapped, enslaved, beaten, murdered, raped, exploited, cheated, traduced, and committed injustice toward a race for over 300 years, how can you escape feelings of guilt, and the fear that they will do to you what you have done to them? A people that can burn a man, cut off his genitals and toes and distribute them for souvenirs, and incarcerate loyal Japanese-Americans in concentrations camps, would have long ago reacted violently to such treatment as they have meted out, and they fear the black man will do what they would have done. They cannot conceive that he can have magnanimity, generosity, and compassion.

So far, there is no prominent black leader advocating such violence, although some have advocated protecting one's self when attacked, as is every man's legal and God-given right. All men are not saints (incidentally, the only way you can become a saint is through martyrdom), and they do not have Martin Luther King Jr.'s saintly qualities and find it hard to look with compassion upon some policeman who is beating their women, or shooting a child, or calling them black sons-of-bitches.

Black Power does not mean violence, but it will give black men a sense of pride and of solidarity and will make them unwilling to continue to bear exploitation.

The direction which Black Power will take depends upon White Power. If White Power acts wisely and with all speedy urgency in making this a livable country for every man, then there will be no reason to fear Black Power.

[1966]

Black Publisher, Black Writer

An Answer

"The truth is that Black publishers cannot publish all Black authors, just as white publishers cannot publish all white authors. There have to be limits measured by literary quality, the publishers' interest, and their financial and editorial capabilities."

John A. Williams has written about the relationships of Black writers with Black publishers (*Black World*, March 1975, Vol. 24, no. 5). He feels that Black publishers have not responded to the disenchantment which Black writers feel about them. I think it's good that he brings this into the open. Perhaps something good can come out of an open, rational discussion.

Mr. Williams says that Black writers are not being published by Black publishers. Then he goes on to name other flaws in Black publishers. He opens many points for discussion, but he makes the questions slippery to handle by not naming names, so that I am not sure exactly what or whom he is talking about. In order that we can be talking about the same things, I must first make a few definitions, to make sure we understand each other, and that one of us will not be talking about bananas while the other is talking about oranges.

First of all, we must eliminate those Black presses which exist to publish the books of only one writer, like Black River Writers or 5X Press. That leaves only a few publishers. The first thing we notice about them is that, like most Black businesses, they are not only small, they are minimal. The largest of them all, Johnson Publishing Company, compared to Harper & Row or McGraw-Hill, is a pigmy. McGraw-Hill could throw away $600,000 on a hoax, Clifford Irving's purportedly authorized biography of Howard Hughes. Compare Harper & Row's publication of 1,426 books in 1972 with Johnson's publication of five. The difference is apparent.

An official of Follett Educational Corporation in a letter to *Publishers Weekly* referred to such small presses as "a kind of 'chickenshack' Black capitalism." Perhaps they are similar in their smallness, but these presses have published some of the best literature today, while McGraw-Hill has thrown away thousands of dollars on some of the worst, like the Clifford Irving hoax.

The Black publishing companies I know best, Third World Press and Jihad Productions, are many times smaller than Johnson Publishing Company. Like most small or underground publishing companies, they were formed to fill a need or to publish a special interest of the publisher. Third World Press was formed to publish the work of certain Black poets of Chicago, Jewel Latimore and Carolyn Rodgers. Those were the first books the press published. In time the press enlarged its scope, but by its deeds you shall know it, and such were its initial deeds. Broadside Press was formed to publish broadsides, selling at 35 cents each. It too enlarged its scope. One of Jihad's first publications was a mimeographed anthology of a Black poetry festival. From such beginnings one can see that these companies did not have the immense capitalization of white companies, which are started by whites having access to loans of $50,000, $100,000, or the backing of immense conglomerates like National General, of which Bantam Books is a division. Nevertheless, even Harper, with its 1,426 titles, rejected the 1,427th. Even Bantam, which publishes 250 paperbacks a month, stops at the 251st. Not only Black authors, but white authors also fail to be published.

These small Black companies were started by poets, not by businessmen. They were not interested in making money, but in publishing what needed to be published. Several years ago a publisher's organization invited Black publishers to hearings, where they could unfold their plans in order to obtain financial or technical help from white publishers or financial institutions. I talked it over with other writers, whose consensus was that it was like standing upon the slave auction block, and I did not attend the hearings. When Roslyn Targ, a literary agent, suggested that I arrange to have Broadside books distributed by a large publisher, I told her no. Don L. Lee likewise rejected an offer by Random House to distribute his books.

All of this is a roundabout way of saying to Mr. Williams that Black publishers are small, under-capitalized (despite all the rantings about Black Capitalism, how are you going to pay your bills unless you have capital), and therefore cannot publish all Black writers who want to be published. Furthermore, Black publishers, like all small publishers, have special idiosyncratic preferences. If Mr. Williams were to present Broadside with a 300-page novel, I'd politely decline, because at this time I am not interested in publishing novels. On the other hand, if he were to submit a 16-page book of poetry as good as his novels, I'd gladly accept it, because my interest is poetry, in small booklets.

Regarding the contracts of Black publishers, the publishers whom I know best are writers themselves and understand writers' feelings. Because of lack of funds, they can't afford to pay advances. In my own contracts, there is no mention of an advance. One writer, who was compiling a dictionary of Black quotations, asked me for an advance to finish her book, but I explained that I couldn't afford to pay advances, and we parted amicably. I did an anthology for Bantam Books and was going to refuse the advance, for I felt uncomfortable at being paid for work I hadn't done. However, my printer advised me I could put the advance in the bank and earn interest on it before the book was published, so I accepted it. What writers may not realize is that an advance is not a gift, but is a pre-payment of future royalties. After my anthology came out, I missed two royalty payments, until the book earned the advances. So what had been paid to me in advance was simply a surfeit before publication in exchange for a dearth after publication. I agree with Mr. Williams that most Black writers would forego advances. I myself am a writer, and neither want nor expect advances.

About delays in publication, again lack of funds of under-capitalized Black publishers is the probable cause. The publisher may owe his printer, and may be loath to get deeper into debt, or perhaps the printer holds up his copy until his debt is reduced. I think the writer should understand this, and be willing to wait. Amos Tutola had to wait six years after acceptance before his best-selling *The Palm Wine Drunkard* was published, and he had a wealthy white publisher. Some authors have a reassuring confidence in their publisher. When I questioned Larry Neal about the delay in publishing his *Black Boogaloo,* he smiled and said, "Joe Goncalves has it, and I know Joe will publish it in good time."

The truth is that Black publishers cannot publish all Black authors, just as white publishers cannot publish all white authors. There have to be limits measured by literary quality, the publishers' interests, and their financial and editorial capabilities. I have set a limit of four books a year, in order to give satisfactory editorial attention and promotion. But last year I published 12. Broadside Press, in its small way, has afforded an outlet for Black writers. In our recently published *Broadside Authors and Artists,* we list 192 persons published by Broadside. If they were not included in individual books, they were contained in our eight anthologies and 89 broadsides.

Regarding the need to sign "major" writers, Gwendolyn Brooks has demonstrated how that is done. She simply decided to leave Harper, although they had been fair to her, because she saw the need to help a Black publisher. I remonstrated with her, warned her that she'd lose money, told her that Broadside Press could give her neither the advances nor the promotion that Harper could, but she insisted on giving a major work, her autobiography, *Report From Part One,* to Broadside Press. When I saw that she was determined, and that if

Broadside Press didn't take the book she would give it to another Black publisher, I gratefully accepted it.

I don't expect or require that all "major" Black writers follow the example of Gwendolyn Brooks, Haki Madhubuti (Don Lee), Sonia Sanchez, or others who have outgrown conventional publishers. These are rare persons, as great in their vision and their courage as in their poetry. Since Black publishers can't publish all Black writers, perhaps it's the writers who have the courage to pioneer, experiment, cooperate, and perhaps sacrifice in determining who should publish with Black publishers. I don't think that Black writers should feel any guilt about publishing with a white publisher. There are more than enough authors to go around.

What are the possibilities of Black publishing? There are 25 million Blacks in this country, a respectably sized nation. Estimate five to a family. That makes five million families. If each of these families bought only one Black book a year, there would be 5 million books sold. Divide that by 100 authors, and that makes an average of 50,000 books for each author. Divide that by 500 authors, and that makes an average of 10,000 books fore each author, a not inconsiderable figure. The problem lies in getting Black folk to read more.

Much has been made of Negroes' oral traditions, as if we were the only people who had them. Oral tradition means only that many people were not able to read or write, and instead of recording things on clay tablets, papyrus, or paper, they passed them down by mouth. Oral tradition has existed wherever people were illiterate—in Appalachia, on the Scottish border, in India, in China. To say Black folk have no capacity to learn to read and write is as silly as saying they don't have enough brains to play football, as was once said to keep Negroes out of the big leagues. The human brain is infinitely flexible. Human beings have enormous capabilities. Black publishers should do all they can to promote reading, like participating in the RIF (Reading Is Fundamental) program, or donating books to schools, churches, prisons, and other institutions. (Some moderation is necessary here. Since we're poor, if we donated too many books we'd go broke.)

I think it's good that Black authors join the authors' Guild. Black publishers, since they are also authors, will join too, and they will learn whatever their authors learn and will adopt whatever will be mutually helpful. Black publishers, since they're also writers, will look with sympathy on authors' wishes about contracts, and will discuss them frankly and truthfully.

Perhaps more Black authors could form cooperatives to publish their work.

Ishmael Reed, Steve Cannon, and Al Young have done just that in California. I agree with Mr. Williams that we should break present publishing practices and make history rather than merely following it. Outgrowing Harper & Row, Gwendolyn Brooks has already made history by selling more than 100,000 books, not once depending on white publishers.

Does Mr. Williams know about the combined Black Publishers, formed in 1972 by Amiri Baraka, Don L. Lee, and other author-publishers? Is Mr. Williams aware of the new Fiction Writers' Cooperative?* Mr. Williams and other authors are invited to be pioneers and innovators and to outgrow traditional methods, as he suggests. This will mean active help to publishers in distributing their books. It may also mean some work and sacrifice on Mr. Williams's part. As I've said, this requires a new breed of author, one who is not content to follow the old ways. Let Mr. Williams bring his new novel to the next meeting of the Combined Black Publishers with the Formentor plan, and we shall see what can be worked out.

[1975]

---

* Formed by a group of novelists who published their own novels. It has been mentioned in *Coda* and *The New Republic* magazine.

Black Poet, White Critic

A critic advises
not to write on controversial subjects
like freedom or murder,
but to treat universal themes
and timeless symbols
like the white unicorn.

A **white** unicorn?

[1965]

The Rite

"Now you must die," the young one said,
"and all your art be overthrown."
The old one only bowed his head
as if those words had been his own.

And with no pity in his eyes
the young man acted out his part
and put him to the sacrifice
and drank his blood and ate his heart.

[1964]

Primitives

Paintings with stiff
homunculus, flat in iron
draperies, with distorted
bodies against spaceless
landscapes

Poems of old
poets in stiff
meters whose harsh
syllables
drag like
dogs with
crushed
backs.

We go back to
them, spurn difficult
grace and
symmetry,
paint tri-faced
monsters,
write lines that
do not sing, or
even croak, but that
bump,
jolt, and are hacked
off in the mid-
dle, as if by these dis-
tortions, this
magic, we can
exorcise
horror, which we
have seen and fear to
see again:

hate deified,
fears and
guilt conquering,
turning cities to
gas, powder and a
little rubble.

[1966]

The Melting Pot

There is a magic melting pot
where any girl or man
can step in Czech or Greek or Scot,
step out American.

Johann and **Jan** and **Jean** and **Juan,**
Giovanni and **Ivan**
step in and then step out again
all freshly christened **John.**

Sam, watching, said, "Why, I was here
even before they came,"
and stepped in too, but was tossed out
before he passed the brim.

And every time Sam tried that pot
they threw him out again.
"Keep out. This is our private pot.
We don't want your black stain."

At last, thrown out a thousand times,
Sam said, "I don't give a damn.
Shove your old pot. You can like it or not,
but I'll be just what I am."

[1968]

Justice

(A Fable)

He fined the Wolf eleven cents
and gave the Lamb ten years in jail.

Langston Blues

Your lips were so laughing
Langston man
Your lips were so singing
Minstrel man
How death could touch them
Hard to understand

Your lips that laughed
And sang so well
Your lips that brought
Laughter from hell
Are silent now
No more to tell

So let us sing
A Langston blues
Sing a lost
Langston blues
Long-gone song
For Langston Hughes

[1967]

Seeds of Revolution

The Revolution
did not begin in 1966
when Stokely raised his fist
and shouted, Black Power.

Nor did it begin last year
when you read Fanon
and discovered you were black.

The Revolution was going on
when the first black
leaped overboard
to the sharks;

When blacks malingered,
or sabotaged the plantation,
or Tommed to outwit Ole Massa;

When your father (whom you deplore)
pushed a broom
and your mother (whom you despise)
scrubbed kitchens
so you could go to school
and read Fanon.

The Revolution
did not begin in 1966
when Stokely raised his fist
and shouted, Black Power.

Nor last year
when you read Fanon
and discovered you were black.

[1969]

An Answer to Lerone Bennett's Questionnaire
On a Name for Black Americans

Discarding the Spanish word for black
and taking the Anglo-Saxon word for Negro,
discarding the names of English slavemasters
and taking the names of Arabian slave-traders
won't put a single
bean in your belly
or an inch of steel
in your spine.

Call a skunk a rose,
and he'll still stink,
and make the name stink too.

Call a rose a skunk,
and it'll still smell sweet,
and even sweeten the name.

The spirit informs the name,
not the name the spirit.

If the white man took the name Negro,
and you took the name Caucasian,
he'd still kick your ass,
as long as you let him.

If you're so insecure
that a word makes you quake
another word
won't cure you.

Change your mind,
not your name.

Change your life,
not your clothes.

[1968]

Put Your Muzzle Where Your Mouth Is
(Or Shut Up)

KILL, KILL, KILL, he screamed.
But when I asked him
(naively, I suppose)
how many
he
had killed,
he said,
Not
1.

[1968]

The Idiot

"That cop was powerful mean.
First, he called me, 'Black boy.'
Then he punched me in the face
and drug me by the collar to a wall
and made me lean against it with my hands on it
while he searched me,
and all the time he searched me
he kicked me and cuffed me and cussed me.

I was hot enough
to lay him out,
and would've did it, only
I didn't want to hurt his feelings,
and lose the good will
of the good white folks downtown,
who hired him."

Informer

He shouted
"Black Power!"
so loudly
we never heard
his whispers
to the F.
B.
I.

F.B.I. Memo

The perfect spy
for the F.B.I.
must have:
beard
Afro
tiki
dashiki
Swahili
and cry
"Kill the honkies!"

Abu

Abu
's a stone black revolutionary.
Decided to blow up City Hall.
Put full-page ad
in *New York Times*
announcing his inten/

                        shun.

Says rightinfrontof
F.B.I. in fil/

              trators
he gon sassinate
rich white liberal
gave only *half*
a million
to N.A.A.C.P.
Says nothing 'bout that Southern sheriff
killed three black prisoners
'cept, he admire him
for his sin/

           cerity.

The Militant Black Poet

A militant black poet
read his scariest poems
to a literary club
of suburban white women.

After the reading
a white-haired lady commented
what a nice man he was,
and that in his place
she'd be much more bitter.

The militant black poet
went home
and *hanged* himself.

Sniper

Somewhere
On a rooftop
You fight for me.

[1967]

Tell It Like It Is

Tell it like it is.
Lies won't get it.
Foaming at the mouth won't get it.
Defamation of character won't get it.

If you want to be virile,
be virile,
but you ain't gonna get virile
by saying somebody else ain't virile.
And if the white boys are all faggots,
like you say,
how come we got all these black poets
with yellow skin?

Beasts

Beasts kill
to live.

Men kill
 for sport
  for love
   for honor
    for bro-ther-hood
    for God
    for red
     white
      and blue.

To praise a man
call him bestial.
To slander beast,
cry, Human!

After the Killing

"We will kill,"
said the blood-thirster,
"and after the killing
there will be peace."

But, after the killing,
their sons
killed his sons,
and his sons
killed their sons,
and their sons
killed his sons

until

at last

a blood-thirster said,
"We will kill.
And after the killing
there will be———peace."

To the Mercy Killers

If ever mercy moves you to murder me,
I pray you, kindly killers, let me live.
Never conspire with death to set me free,
but let me know such life as pain can give.
Even though I be a clot, an aching clench,
a stub, a stump, a butt, a scab, a knob,
a screaming pain, a putrefying stench,
still let me live, so long as life shall throb.
Even though I turn such traitor to myself
as beg to die, do not accomplice me.
Even though I seem not human, a mute shelf
of glucose, bottled blood, machinery
to swell the lung and pump the heart—even so,
do not put out my life. Let me still glow.

[1963]

Ancestors

Why are our ancestors
Always kings or princes
And never the common people?

Was the Old Country a democracy
where every man was a king?
Or did the slavecatchers
steal only the aristocrats
and leave the fieldhands
laborers
streetcleaners
garbage collectors
dishwashers
cooks
and maids
behind?

My own ancestor
(research reveals)
was a swineherd,
who tended the pigs
in the Royal Pigstye
and slept in the mud
among the hogs.

Yet I'm as proud of him
as of any king or prince
dreamed up in fantasies
of bygone glory.

[1970]

A Different Image

The age
requires this task:
create
a different image;
re-animate
the mask.

Shatter the icons of slavery and fear.
Replace
the leer
of the minstrel's burnt-cork face
with a proud, serene
and classic bronze of Benin.

[1970]

In Africa

In Africa, in Africa
the strangers came and took the gold,
the emeralds and the diamonds,
the ivory and the slaves,
and paid for them in beads of glass
and cotton cloth and rum and gin.

In Africa in Africa
the strangers come & take the gold
& copper & petroleum
& bauxite & uranium
& pay for them with bicycles
& motor bikes & Citroens
& cinema & gin.

[1970, 1980]

African Suite

1
Slave Castle
(ELMINA, GHANA 1970)

Some were crying
   and some were cursing
Some were dry-eyed
   and some said never a
   mumbalin word

      when we stopped in the dark dungeons
      felt the chains and manacles
      stared at the cold grey waters
      tossing to frightful shores

Some were crying
some were cursing
some were dry-eyed
some said never a
mumbalin word

2
Hotel Continental
(ACCRA, GHANA)

Africa's
not considered
a continent
here.
While Europeans,
Americans,
Asians
dine,
the only Africans
in the room
are waiters.

3
Hotel Ivoire
(ABIDJAN, IVORY COAST)

Outside the hotel
a beautiful black girl
in a white bikini
lolls
in a billboard.

If she should step out of the billboard
to swim in the hotel pool,
she would gash her feet
on the broken glass
set in the concrete fence
the French erected
to keep the Africans
OUT.

4
Village Girl
(AMASAMAN, GHANA)

Your black is deep
against the blue and white of your robe.
Your eyes are moons
in midnight Ghana sky.
The gems in your ears
are stars.

[1970]

Black Emotion and Experience

The Literature for Understanding

In 1970 I took movies of black American students coming out of the dungeons of the former slave castle in Elmina, Ghana. The tour of the castle was a profoundly moving experience for us. Probably all of us thought, "Long ago our mothers and fathers passed through just such a place as this. People like us suffered and died here." Our emotional upheaval was evident in facial expressions, gestures   words   tears.

> Some were crying
>   and some were cursing
> Some were dry-eyed
>   and some said never a
>   mumbalin word

There were also white American students in the group, but perhaps they were not so deeply affected. Perhaps they reflected on man's inhumanity to man, but doubtless none of them thought, "I was a slave here, long ago." As all of us looked over the parapets at the cold gray Atlantic and thought of America far away, our thoughts of our ancestors who crossed those waters had to be different. The ancestors of the white students probably had some foreboding of a strange land, of physical hardships, of natives who might resent having their land taken from them, but mostly they had a sense of freedom—freedom from religious and political persecution, freedom from famine, from debt, from jail, freedom to achieve a new and prosperous life. On the other hand, the ancestors of the black students were kidnapped from their traditional culture to a land which they could consider only with horror and fright.

This qualitative difference of emotion and experience is what strikes one in black American literature. Not only was there a difference in the way blacks came here, there is also a difference in the way blacks regard American myths and heroes. Whites revere George Washington of the cherry tree incident. Black poet June Jordan says, "George Washington he think he big / he trade my father for a pig." Some people are shocked and disturbed, especially by the younger writers of today. "Why the propaganda, the obscenity, the violence, the hate, the rage?"

One white critic, David Littlejohn, in his book *Black on White,* describes black literature as a race war. Hoyt W. Fuller, editor of *Black World,* advised readers not to touch the book, although Littlejohn's evaluations of many of the writers are similar to Fuller's own judgments of their work. What Fuller objects to is Littlejohn's characterization of black writers as mean-spirited if they show anger and resentment instead of philosophical benignity. Fuller maintains that the anger is justified, and that Littlejohn's objections only show the critic's guilt and his inability to handle it.

Nevertheless, in order to understand the black experience, one must read such works. For works of literature such as poems, plays, stories, essays, and biographies force one to feel intense emotions and thus get inside the experience, whereas factual books of history, sociology, and economics afford a merely intellectual approach.

I won't attempt to cram the history of black American literature into a few pages, or to chronicle the first, or even the best, work or works in different genres. I'll select a few works in which one can relive portions of the black experience in America, and will list anthologies and bibliographies that one can explore for further reading.

Only a minority of the works are of the type that disturb some readers. Early black writers had to please white editors and readers or remain unpublished and unread. Besides, the black experience is not one, but many. There is W. E. B. Du Bois, born in Massachusetts and educated at Fisk, Harvard, and the University of Berlin. There is Richard Wright, born in Mississippi, who started drinking as a child, with little formal education, but dying, like Du Bois, in exile. There is the sharecropper in Georgia, there is the porter in Harlem, there is the factory worker in Detroit. But through all these varied experiences, violence, suffering, and injustice, mammoth to petty, run like a red thread.

It is evident in the earliest compositions, the folk poetry. Du Bois called the spirituals the Sorrow songs and praised their music while calling much of their verse doggerel. But the poetry was refined as well as debased by passing through the oral tradition. Even the titles are poetry—"Deep River," "I Got a Home in Dat Rock," "Gamblin Man, Get Off Yo Knees"—and there are many startlingly fine lines ("Dark midnight was my cry"); stanzas of monumental dignity in "Crucifixion" and "Were You There When They Crucified My Lord"; and almost perfect lyrics in "I Know de Moonlight" and "No More Auction Block." James Weldon Johnson and J. Rosamond Johnson's *The Book of American Negro Spirituals* contains both texts and music of many spirituals, with an introduction on their dialect, music, and origins. Both religious and secular folk poetry can be found in Sterling Brown's *Negro Caravan* and Dudley Randall's *The Black Poets*.

A good collection of secular folk poetry containing blues, ballads, work songs, and humorous lyrics is Thomas Washington Talley's *Negro Folk Rhymes*. A. Xavier Nicholas has collected the songs of some of the singers of our own day—Chuck Berry, James Brown, Curtis Mayfield, Nina Simone, and others in *The Poetry of Soul*.

A poet whose *Collected Poems* has never been out of print is Paul Laurence Dunbar. He is best known for his dialect verse which presents a rose-tinted picture of plantation life with pathos and humor. His Standard English verse, which he himself preferred, is by no means negligible. His rondeau "We Wear the Mask" sounds a theme which often recurs in black poetry. His largely white audience preferred his dialect verse, however. James Weldon Johnson's *God's Trombones: Seven Negro Sermons in Verse* suggests the eloquence of the old-time black preachers, not with misspelled words, but through syntax, diction, and rural images.

The predicament of Dunbar is one in which most black authors have found themselves. Until the 1960s, with the emergence of black publishers, black magazines, black bookstores, and a black audience, black writers have had to address themselves to a largely white audience, through white magazines and white editors and publishers. If white editors thought a book was too militant, or would not interest white readers, the author was told to tone down his message, or the book was rejected. Also, black books were regarded as a special category, like detective stories. If the publisher had his quota of black books, he would accept no more.

The decade of the 1920s, the Harlem Renaissance, saw a group of talented writers with a heightened race pride and awareness of their African heritage. Claude McKay was the forerunner with his famous sonnet "If We Must Die," which was widely read and declaimed during the post–World War I riots, quoted by Winston Churchill to the United States Congress in World War II, and in 1971 passed around among the prisoners before the Attica prison riot. A *Time* magazine correspondent called it "a poem written by an unknown prisoner, crude but touching in its would-be heroic style." This put-down of the famous, classic sonnet provoked an avalanche of letters to *Time* magazine. Langston Hughes, called the poet laureate of Harlem, presented the night clubs, the streets, the men and women of Harlem with humor and sympathy in many verses which can be found in his *Selected Poems*. Jean Toomer's *Cane* was one of the most important books to come out of the Harlem Renaissance. It is a collection of sketches, short stories, poems, and a play, in language whose images and symbols are richly evocative. Countee Cullen's verse was traditional but polished. Sterling Brown's dramatic and humorous ballads and blues are a rural counterpart to Hughes's urban poetry.

Like Hughes, Gwendolyn Brooks writes about the blacks of the city. She presents the people of Chicago's South Side in richly textured verse. She is a pleasure to read not only for the humanity of her poems but for their skilled craftsmanship. Her books of poetry and her novel *Maud Martha* have been collected in *The World of Gwendolyn Brooks*. Another skilled and sensitive poet is Robert Hayden whose *Selected Poems* was published in 1966.

One of the most influential poets today is Imamu Amiri Baraka (formerly LeRoi Jones). Originally a poet of the Greenwich Village school, he left New York and settled in his birthplace, Newark, established Spirit House and a black theatre, and engaged in local politics and recently helped to form the National Black Political Convention. He is one of the founders of the Black Arts movement, and his famous poem, "Black Art," is a manifesto of the ideology that art should be functional and should effect social change. It appears in his *Black Magic Poems*.

During the sixties small black publishing firms sprang up, joining the older Associate Publishers and Johnson Publishing Company. They found a wide black audience, stimulated by the civil rights struggle intensified in the fifties. Many of the readers were young—college students or even high school students. Most of the publishers were writers themselves. Poet Amiri Baraka founded Jihad Productions in Newark. Poet Dudley Randall founded Broadside Press in Detroit. Poet Don L. Lee established Third World Press in Chicago. Drum and Spear Press was established in Washington, D.C. Editor Alfred Prettyman founded Emerson Hall Press in New York. Far from censoring black authors, the new publishers encouraged them to speak to and for black people, to express their fury and frustration, their love and longing.

A remarkable group of poets was published by Broadside Press. Most of them can be found in Gwendolyn Brooks's *A Broadside Treasury* 1965–1970. Don L. Lee in *Think Black* asserted, "I was born into slavery in February of 1942. In the spring of that same year 110,000 persons of Japanese descent were placed in protective custody by the white people of the United States. . . . World War II, the war against racism; yet no Germans or other enemy aliens were placed in protective custody. There should have been Japanese writers directing their writings toward Japanese audiences. Black. Poet. Black poet am I. This should leave little doubt in the minds of anyone as to which is first." Lee exhorted his audiences to "change," and to "know your enemy, the real enemy." Nikki Giovanni asked, in *Black Feeling, Black Talk*,

Can you kill . . .
Can you piss on a blond head
Can you cut it off . . .
Can you lure them to bed to kill them

Sonia Sanchez wrote in "Malcolm"

yet this man
this dreamer,
thick-lipped with words
will never speak again
and in each winter
when the cold air cracks
with frost, I'll breathe
his breath and mourn
my gun-filled nights.

Etheridge Knight wrote *Poems from Prison* while an inmate in Indiana State Prison. He does not pose as self-righteous, but admits his vulnerability like ours, and his poems about black prisoners and himself are powerful and moving. He has edited a book of prison writings, *Black Voices from Prison*, which is one of the earliest of the prison anthologies.

There were so many poets in the 1960s that they have been said to constitute another Harlem Renaissance. It would be tedious to list them all, but they and earlier poets can be found in the anthologies which proliferated in the sixties, some of which are listed, with previous anthologies, in roughly chronological order: Robert Thomas Kerlin's *Negro Poets and Their Poems*, Countee Cullen's *Caroling Dusk*, James Weldon Johnson's *The Book of American Negro Poetry*, Arna Bontemps and Langston Hughes's *Poetry of the Negro*, Paul Breman's *Sixes and Sevens*, Rosey E. Pool's *Beyond the Blues* and *Ik Ben die Nieuwe Neger*, Arna Bontemp's *American Negro Poetry*, Langston Hughes's *New Negro Poets:*

U.S.A., Dudley Randall and Margaret G. Burroughs's *For Malcolm,* Robert Hayden's *Kaleidoscope,* Clarence Major's *The New Black Poetry,* Adam Miller's *Dice or Black Bones,* Dudley Randall's *Black Poetry* and *The Black Poets,* Orde Coombs's *We Speak as Liberators,* June Jordan's *Soul Script,* Ted Wilentz and Tom Weatherly's *Natural Process,* Jill Witherspoon's *A Broadside Annual 1972,* Bernard Bell's *Modern and Contemporary Afro-American Poetry.*

The anthology *Black Fire,* edited by LeRoi Jones and Larry Neal, is a collection similar in its importance for the sixties to Brown, Davis, and Lee's *Negro Caravan* for its importance to the period up to 1940. It presents poems, stories, essays, and plays of the revolutionary young black writers of the sixties. Ahmed Alhamisi and Harun Kofi Wangara's *Black Arts: An Anthology of Black Creations* is a collection of similar intent to that of *Black Fire,* but in addition to writings it also contains graphics.

Poetry, because of its brevity and expressiveness, and the speed and inexpensiveness with which it can be composed and published in contrast to the slowness and cost of novels and plays, has been the most popular literary art among black Americans. I'll name a few works in the other forms, however, by which one can feel his way into the black experience.

Similar to poetry in their brevity, immediacy, and impact are essays, of which there have been many fine writers. W. E. B. Du Bois's *Souls of Black Folk* is influential for its insights and prophecies, dissecting the Booker Washington fallacy, expressing the double consciousness of the Negro, pinpointing the color-line as the problem of the twentieth century, recommending federal aid for education. James Baldwin's sensitive essays trace the growth of his black consciousness from *Notes of a Native Son, Nobody Knows My Name,* and *The Fire Next Time* to *No Name in the Street.* The same kind of growth is seen in Amiri Baraka's *Home,* culminating in *Raise Race Rays Raze: Essays since 1965.* Eldridge Cleaver's *Soul on Ice* has eloquent essays on his prison experiences and introspections. George Jackson's letters in *Soledad Brother* reveal prison conditions and his indomitable reaction to them. Ralph Ellison's *Shadow and Act* contains his reflections on music and literature. Poet Don L. Lee's first book of essays, *From Plan to Planet,* is concerned with Pan-Africanism and black literature.

A special Negro form of biography is the slave narrative, often written as abolitionist propaganda. Outstanding among these for its clear, direct style and its insight into the effects of slavery on slave and slaveholder alike is Frederick Douglass's *Narrative of the Life of Frederick Douglass.* In sharp contrast is Booker T. Washington's *Up from Slavery,* which is an Horatio Alger type of biography with homilies and many reports of compliments paid him by prominent whites. Richard Wright's *Black Boy* also concerns growing up in the South, but it presents a much harsher picture.

The Autobiography of Malcolm X, as told to Alex Haley, has profoundly influenced the attitudes of blacks. It is epic, as it describes Malcolm's transformation from small-town boy, big-city hustler, and prisoner to minister, leader, and martyr. Chester Himes's *The Quality of Hurt* is valuable for its account of the black expatriate writer's life in Europe and his relations with Richard Wright and other expatriates. It does not satisfy our curiosity about his craft of writing, but it intrigues us with his intensity of living. Many blacks have been angered by refusal of service in a restaurant, but it was Chester Himes who jumped on the counter and pistol whipped the proprietor on the head. Gwendolyn Brooks's *Report from Part One* is a writer's autobiography which tells us much about her art. There are explications of her novel and of some of her poems, and two interviews about her writing.

I've just noticed that most of these books are autobiographies, except perhaps the "as-told-to" Malcolm X book. It's curious that those biographies which convey a special flavor of the black experience are mostly autobiographies. As I think of additional books, it is still autobiographies that come to mind, like *The Autobiography of W. E. B. Du Bois,* Claude Brown's *Manchild in the Promised Land,* or Piri Thomas's *Down These Mean Streets.* Perhaps black poets and novelists should write biographies also, to impart to them their special insight and skill which would make the story of a life memorable.

The outstanding works of fiction are easy to identify. The two that tower over all the rest are Richard Wright's *Native Son* and Ralph Ellison's *Invisible Man. Native Son* liberated succeeding writers by portraying Bigger Thomas who hated and feared whites and who gained a sense of self only when he took responsibility for an act of violence. After Wright, black novelists no longer hesitated to portray violent emotions. *Invisible Man* is rich in language, incident, irony, humor, symbols, levels of meaning. It adumbrates the black experience in education, industry, labor unions, the Communist Party, black nationalism. William Demby in *Bettlecreek,* the story of a white recluse and black adolescents in a southern town, has used images and symbols to suggest added emotional dimensions. Ishmael Reed in *Mumbo Jumbo* makes a surrealist mixture of fantasy, history, satire, and voodoo. But most of the successors of Wright and Ellison have followed Wright in the path of realism. John A.

Williams's *The Man Who Cried I Am* is a panoramic novel which follows a writer from America to Europe and involves characters in the black expatriate scene and in American and European plans of concentration camps and genocide for blacks. Williams's most recent book, *Captain Blackman,* follows the memories of a wounded soldier in Vietnam through all the wars since the Revolutionary War in which black soldiers have been involved, with all the irony and disillusionment of fighting for others' freedom but not for their own. Another historical novel, a black counterpart to *Gone with the Wind,* is Margaret Walker's *Jubilee,* based on the life of her grandmother during the Civil War and Reconstruction. Cyrus Colter's short stories in *The Beach Umbrella* probe the lives of a wide range of characters in Chicago's black South Side. James Alan McPherson in *Hue and Cry* has also shown mastery of the short story. His story "A Solo Song: For Doc" brings to vivid life again the almost forgotten ambience of the railroad dining car and the working conditions of the black dining car waiter.

There have been many good black actors, but black playwrights have been scarce. In the sixties, however, there appeared a profusion of playwrights like that of poets. Joining the older dramatists like Langston Hughes, Alice Childress, Loften Mitchell, William Branch, there appeared Lorraine Hansberry, Ossie Davis, Amiri Baraka, James Baldwin, Ed Bullins, Charles Gordone, Marvin X, Jimmy Garrett, Sonia Sanchez, Lonne Elder III, Ronald Milner, Melvin Van Peebles, and Ben Caldwell.

Promoting the rise of theatre was the Black Arts movement fostered by Amiri Baraka and others, which stimulated the growth of local theatres throughout the country.

Lorraine Hansberry's *Raisin in the Sun* is a well-made play of black family life. Ossie Davis's *Purlie Victorious* is a farce satirizing obvious racial stereotypes in the South. Amiri Baraka's *The Dutchman* is a tense one-act play showing a confrontation between a white woman and a young middle-class black man in a subway car. These and other plays can be found in single volumes or in the collections *Black Theatre,* by Linda Patterson, *Black Drama Anthology,* by Woodie King and Ronald Milner, *New Black Playwrights,* by William Couch, or Ed Bullins's *New Plays from the Black Theatre.*

Much of the literature of the 1960s was first published in black magazines, and they are useful for discerning trends. *The Journal of Black Poetry* is a leading poetry magazine. *Freedomways* is distinguished by its long annotated booklists prepared by librarian Ernest Kaiser. *Dasein, Liberator, Soulbook, Black Dialogue,* and *Umbra* were literary magazines that flourished in the sixties, but they seem to be dormant now. Recent magazines of quality are *Black Scholar* and *Black Creation,* which carry articles and interviews on new trends and persons in the arts; *Essence,* a woman's magazine which features good poetry; and *Encore,* a monthly of worldwide news of interest to blacks, which recently featured a story on black soldiers in the Ulster troubles and a conversation between poets Nikki Giovanni and Yevgeny Yevtushenko. *Black World* has published many young writers whose contributions appeared later in books. The magazine has annual poetry, drama, and fiction numbers, and has had special issues on the Harlem Renaissance, Richard Wright, and the Black Aesthetic.

There has been much discussion of the Black Aesthetic. In *Black World's* symposium on the Black Aesthetic in 1968, some writers had never heard of it. On the other hand, Margaret Walker said, "The 'black aesthetic' has a rich if undiscovered past. This goes back in time to the beginnings of civilization in Egypt, Babylonia, India, China, Persia, and all the Islamic world that precedes the Renaissance of the Europeans." The following points may give some idea of what is generally agreed on by its proponents:

1. It is not wise to try to define the Black Aesthetic too narrowly at this time, as too rigid definition may restrict its development. After further development of black literature, it may be described, not prescribed, by observing the literature created under its influence.
2. Black art should be functional, not decorative.
3. The function of black art is to unify and liberate black people all over the world.
4. Black art should create positive concepts, images, and symbols for black folk, and destroy negative ones, i.e., black is beautiful, not ugly or filthy.
5. In creating new images and concepts, writers may change or reverse the language of the oppressor, using black idioms. When Sonia Sanchez says, "We a baddDDD people," she means, "We a great people."
6. Black art should be directed to black people for black people. The reactions of white critics and readers are irrelevant.

Addison Gayle's *The Black Aesthetic* is an anthology of critical essays on the Black Aesthetic in the various arts. His earlier anthology, *Black Expressions,* is a collection of essays on black literature, written from the 1920s to the 1960s.

Alain Locke's *The New Negro* is an anthology which helped to launch the Harlem Renaissance. Nathan Irving Huggins's *Harlem Renaissance* is a recent in-depth study of the period. Sterling Brown's *The Negro in American Fiction: Negro Poetry and Drama* and Jay Saunders Redding's *To Make a Poet Black* are two works of criticism of both prose and poetry. Widening its scope from poetry to prose, Broadside Press has started a *Broadside Critics Series,* featuring black critics on black poets. The first volume is *Dynamite Voices: Black Poets of the 1960s,* by Don L. Lee. The second is *Claude McKay: The Black Poet at War,* by Addison Gayle. *The Militant Black Writer in Africa and the United States,* by Mercer Cook and Stephen E. Henderson, discusses the younger African and Afro-American writers. Ezekiel Mphalele's *Voices in the Whirlwind* examines both Afro-American and African poets, and analyzes the Black Aesthetic to see what is in it, which is not covered by other aesthetic canons. Harold Cruse's *The Crisis of the Negro Intellectual* blames Negro artists for not building a solid foundation for their art by creating black institutions. A book which is not criticism, but which may help readers to understand some of the language which they will encounter, especially in the new black poetry, is J. L. Dillard's *Black English.* Dillard shows that black English is not incorrect English, but a dialect of English, with its roots in West African languages and with its own syntax and grammar.

Poetry has been perhaps the most popular literary form, not only because it is the fastest and least expensive to create and to reproduce, but also because it is in the black oral tradition. The jazz musician, for instance, is a contemporary culture hero of black poets. Perhaps more poems have been written about John Coltrane than about any other black figure except Malcolm X. Collaboration between the poet and the musician has been abrogated. Imagine James Brown performing a lyric of Don Lee. Nina Simone has already set to music and recorded Langston Hughes's "Blacklash Blues."

Because of the prevalence of the oral tradition, Amiri Baraka in the April 1972 *Black World* advised young poets to write plays and skits, and to perform them in theatres, churches, and schools. Most black people, however, have not formed the habit of going to the theatre at 8:30 p.m. Blacks do attend movies, however, and their interest in the new black films has revivified a dying movie industry. But most of the new films, except for a few like *Buck and the Preacher,* have exploited sex and dope, and have been vehemently criticized by segments of the black community. If the many good poets and playwrights now working, instead of commercial hacks, were to write movie scripts, perhaps fine work might be produced. Financing is the greatest obstacle. But just imagine a movie produced by Motown, starring Sidney Poitier and Ruby Dee, directed by Gordon Parks, with a script by Amiri Baraka, out of a story by Ralph Ellison. It might even be rerun on television!

[1973]

THE LAST LEAP OF THE MUSE

A Poet Is Not a Jukebox

A poet is not a jukebox, so don't tell me what to write.
I read a dear friend a poem about love, and she said,
"You're in to that bag now, for whatever it's worth,
But why don't you write about the riot in Miami?"

I didn't write about Miami because I didn't know about Miami.
I've been so busy working for the Census, and listening to music all night, and
    making new poems
That I've broken my habit of watching TV and reading newspapers.
So it wasn't absence of Black Pride that caused me not to write about Miami,
But simple ignorance.

Telling a Black poet what he ought to write
Is like some Commissar of Culture in Russia telling a poet
He'd better write about the new steel furnaces in the Novobigorsk region,
Or the heroic feats of Soviet labor in digging the trans-Caucasus Canal,
Or the unprecedented achievement of workers in the sugar beet industry who
    exceeded their quota by 400 per cent (it was later discovered to be a typist's
    error).

Maybe the Russian poet is watching his mother die of cancer,
Or is bleeding from an unhappy love affair,
Or is bursting with happiness and wants to sing of wine, roses, nightingales.

I'll bet that in a hundred years the poems the Russian people will read, sing,
    and love
Will be the poems about his mother's death, his unfaithful mistress, or his
    wine, roses and nightingales,
Not the poems about steel furnaces, the trans-Caucasus Canal, or the sugar
    beet industry.
A poet writes about what he feels, what agitates his heart and sets his pen in
    motion.
Not what some apparatchik dictates, to promote his own career or theories.

Yeah, maybe I'll write about Miami, as I wrote about Birmingham.
But it'll be because I want to write about Miami, not because somebody says
    I ought to.

Yeah, I write about love. What's wrong with love?
If we had more loving, we'd have more Black babies to become Black brothers
    and sisters and build the Black family.

When people love, they bathe with sweet-smelling soap, splash their bodies
    with perfume or cologne,
Shave, and comb their hair, and put on gleaming silken garments,
Speak softly and kindly and study their beloved to anticipate and satisfy her
    every desire.
After loving they're relaxed and happy and friends with all the world.
What's wrong with love, beauty, joy, or peace?

If Josephine had given Napoleon more loving, he wouldn't have sown the
    meadows of Europe with skulls.
If Hitler had been happy in love, he wouldn't have baked people in ovens.
So don't tell me it's trivial and a cop-out to write about love and not about
    Miami.

A poet is not a jukebox.
A poet is not a jukebox.
I repeat, A poet is not a jukebox for someone to shove a quarter in his ear and
    get the tune they want to hear.
Or to pat on the head and call "a good little Revolutionary."
Or to give a Kuumba Liberation Award.

A poet is not a *jukebox*.
A poet is *not* a jukebox.
A *poet* is not a jukebox.

So don't tell *me* what to write.

[1980]

My Muse

I never thought I'd have a Muse.
Then I met you.
Now poems gush in an unending stream,
Inspired by you.

Sometimes in tenderness,
Sometimes in wrath,
The poems pour forth.

To me you are Catullus's Lesbia,
Shakespeare's Dark Lady,
Dante's Beatrice,
Poe's Annabel Lee,
My Zasha.

My Zasha,
Who makes the poems pour forth.

Zasha, of the tall slim dancer's body,
The dark face,
The dark voice,
The narrow, sidelong-glancing eyes.

My Zasha,
She Devil,
Who spews forth filth when she is questioned,
And carries a butcher knife in her purse.

[1980]

Translation from Chopin

(Prelude Number 7 in A Major, Opus 28)

If I should say to you
That I have loved you long
With love that's sweet and true
And like a tender song,
If you should say to me
That you have loved me too,
Then all my life would be
A symphony to you.

If I had loved you less,
Or you had loved me more,
This pain and loneliness
Would never pierce my core.
If I had loved you less,
Or you had cared for me,
I never would have wept,
My pain would never be.

[1980]

Detroit Renaissance

(For Mayor Coleman A. Young)

Cities have died, have burned,
yet phoenix-like returned
to soar up livelier, lovelier than before.
Detroit has felt the fire,
Yet each time left the pyre
As if the flames had power to restore.

First, burn away the myths
Of what it was, and is—
A lovely, tree-lined town of peace and trade.
Hatred has festered here,
And bigotry and fear
Filled streets with strife and raised the barricade.

Wealth of a city lies
Not in its factories,
Its marts and towers crowding to the sky,
But in its people, who
Possess grace to imbue
Their lives with beauty, wisdom, charity.

You have those, too long hid,
Who built the pyramids,
Who searched the skies and mapped the planets' range,
Who sang the songs of grief
That made the whole world weep,
Whose Douglass, Malcolm, Martin rung in change;

The Indian, with his soul
Attuned to Nature's role;
The sons and daughters of Cervantes' smile;
Pan Tadeusz's children too
Entrust their fate to you;
Souls forged by Homer's, Dante's, Shakespeare's, Goethe's, Yeats's style.

Together we will build
A city that will yield
To all their hopes and dreams so long deferred.
New faces will appear
Too long neglected here;
New minds, new means will build a brave new world.

[1980]

Bag Woman

(For Jane Hale Morgan)

Wearing an overcoat in August heat,
Shawls and scarves, a torn and dirty dress,
Newspaper shoes, she squats in the Greyhound terminal
And rummages through two bags, her lifetime treasure.

She mines waste baskets for her food and clothes,
Forages in the streets with sparrows, pigeons—
Isolate, with fewer friends than beggars have—
Another stray cat or abandoned dog,
She sleeps where cats and dogs sleep, in the streets.

Sister, once did you suck your mother's milk,
And laugh as she fondled you? Did Daddy
Call you his Dumpling, Baby Girl, his Princess?
And did you flirt with him, bending your head,
And, giggling, kiss his eyes through your long lashes?
Did some boy love you once, and hold you tight,
And hotly know you through a summer night?

Or were you gang-raped, violated early,
And from that trauma drifted down to this?
Or, born defective, abandoned to the streets?

Sister, I do not know. But I know that I am you.
I touch your rags, clasp your dumb eyes.
Talk with you, and drink your fetid breath.

[1980]

The Aging Whore

White wig askew above black face,
She totters on high heels up Woodward Avenue
Waving her hands above her head,
Cutting dance steps to Ella's scatting
Over radio from a MacDonald's hamburger palace.

She wears a tan blouse with belly bulging farther than her breasts.
Baggy blue pants with rubber bands below the knees
To accentuate her legs. No longer a stripling
In tight skirt slit to the crotch,
Or crisp, hip-hugging slacks, black men ignore her.
They can get younger trim for nothing.

She ignores them, but flags the passing cars.
Perhaps some lonely and aging white from the suburbs,
Whom Puritans have taught that sex is grotesque,
Will stop his car and bargain with her.

But no one stops. Tired,
She sinks to the bench outside MacDonald's.

A spent, wornout woman,
With vestiges of a once winsome face,
You can see why her pimp
Praised, petted, and marketed her. Now, we pity,
As she spews hate
(Don't let no man touch you.
Don't give 'em nothing.)
In accents scabbed with obscenities
Once the daring darts of a reckless girl,
Now the filth of a young-old harridan,
Which spatters the shocked faces
Of women and school girls
Stopped at the curb by the red light.

[1981]

Poor Dumb Butch

Poor Dumb Butch,
Whom at first we called Wrinkle because of the white line that cavorted
    from your brow to your snout,
Who looked like a bear cub as a puppy and grew into a pony
Who knocked us down as you reared on your hind legs to welcome us,
Who scored 20 out of a possible 200 on your final exam in obedience
    training.

Poor Dumb Butch,
Yet you were better than I was.
You always outboxed me when I fought and wrestled with you,
Although your only fist was your slender nose,
And outran me when we chased each other around the yard,
And were always eager to walk with me through snow or rain,
And when in pain and incurably sick in your old age I took you to the
    veterinarian to kill you,
Your eyes glowed with love and anticipation as I fastened your leash.

[1980]

To an Old Man

(An Easter gift for James Barnett Spencer
and Vivian Barnett Spencer Randall)

The deadweight of your body in my arms
I muscle up as once you hefted me.
Your bleared red eyes that roll and scarcely see
once focused gently on my infant form.
Your shit, piss, phlegm, sweat, tears I wipe away
as once you washed my body as a child.
Your hand rigid and still or shaking wild
once held my hand, restrained when I would stray.

There was a girl who cried for a garden pool,
and your numb fingers nimbly fashioned one.
Their craft and all their cunning long since gone,
they balk at buttons, vainly pluck and pull.
O diapered old man, you're now a child,
your child your parent. Talk with me a while.

[1980]

AFTERWORD

Happiness

Happiness
is a capricious girl.
Woo her, she flees.
Ignore her, she follows.

When I was young and alone,
Sundays I stayed in my room all day
making poetry on the card table, and Tottie,
hearing no sound, would tap on the door and ask,
"Are you all right?" And when I answered,
she'd go down to the kitchen and bring me
sandwiches and milk.

I never thought that I was happy then.
But now when I look back, I know
I was very happy.

[1944]

APPENDIX 1: POETRY BOOKS BY DUDLEY RANDALL, WITH CONTENTS

Poem Counterpoem (1966)
Ballad of Birmingham
Memorial Wreath
Booker T. and W. E. B.
Old Witherington
The Southern Road
Legacy: My South
For Margaret Danner
George
Souvenirs
Belle Isle

Cities Burning (1968)
Roses and Revolutions
Primitives
The Rite
Black Poet, White Critic
Hail, Dionysos
Analysands
Dressed All in Pink
Ballad of Birmingham
The Idiot
The Melting Pot

A Different Image
Augury for an Infant

Love You (1970)
 The Profile on the Pillow
 And Why the Softness
 Goddess of Love
 Good to Be in You
 The Gift
 Thunderstorm
 Black Magic
 Faces
 Meeting
 The Brightness Moved Us Softly
 At the Post House
 Love Poem
 My Second Birth
 Sanctuary

More to Remember (1970)
 1 The Kindness and the Cruelty
 For Pharish Pinckney, Bindle-Stiff during the Depression
 Vacant Lot
 Ghetto Girls
 Laughter in the Slums
 Winter Campus: Ann Arbor
 Shape of the Invisible
 Nocturne
 2 Incredible Harvests
 Our Name for You
 Separation
 Rx
 The Line-Up
 Jailhouse Blues
 The Apparition
 Perspectives
 Spring before a War

Helmeted Boy
Football Season
Lost in the Mails
Pacific Epitaphs
    Rabaul
    New Georgia
    Treasury Islands
    Palawan
    Espiritu Santu
    Iwo Jima
    Bismarck Sea
    Tarawa
    Halmaherra
    New Guinea
    Luzon
    Coral Sea
    Bougainville
    Vella Vella
    Leyte
    Guadalcanal
    Borneo
The Ascent
Coral Atoll
The Leaders

3 If Not Attic, Alexandrian
Interview
The Dilemma
Aim
Love Song
April Mood
Anniversary Words

4 And Her Skin Deep Velvet Night
Poet
Aphorisms
Hymn

The Trouble with Intellectuals
The Intellectuals
Poem, on a Nude, from the Ballet, to Debussy's Prelude *L'Après-Midi D'un Faune,* after Mallarmé's *L'Après-Midi D'un Faune*
Justice (A Fable)
Mainly by the Music
Langston Blues
Straight Talk from a Patriot
Daily News Report
Seeds of Revolution
An Answer to Lerone Bennett's Questionnaire On a Name for Black Americans
Nationalist
Put Your Muzzle Where Your Mouth Is (Or Shut Up)
Informer
F.B.I. Memo
Abu
The Militant Black Poet
Sniper
Ancestors
On Getting a Natural

After the Killing (1973)
African Suite
Tell It Like It Is
Words Words Words
Beasts
After the Killing
To the Mercy Killers
Frederick Douglass and the Slave Breaker
Courage
To William T. Patrick, Jr.
For Gwendolyn Brooks, Teacher
Miracle
The Flight
A Marriage
Green Apples
I Loved You Once

A Litany of Friends (1981)

I. Friends

A Litany of Friends

George

Poor Dumb Butch

For Pharish Pinckney, Bindle-Stiff during the Depression

Old Witherington

The Happy Painter

To an Old Man

For My Students

My Students

The Six

Langston Blues

For Margaret Danner

For Gwendolyn Brooks, Teacher

On Getting a Natural

II. Eros

The Ones I Love

Souvenirs

Perspectives

Anniversary Words

A Marriage

Sweet Breathed Celia

The Future Looms

The Flight

The Profile on the Pillow

Loss

The Mini Skirt

Impromptus

My Muse

To be in Love

A Warning

A Plea

Maiden, Open

To a Mother

If I Were God I'd

My Verse That Once Was Tender
May and December: A Song
Translation from Chopin
Women
The New Woman
I Loved You Once (Ya Vas Lyubil)
The Erotic Poetry of Sir Isaac Newton

III. War
Spring before a War
Helmeted Boy
Lost in the Mails
Games
Daily News Report
Straight Talk from a Patriot
Coral Atoll
Pacific Epitaphs
The Ascent
Wait for Me (Zhdi Myenya)
My Native Land (Rodina)

IV. Africa
In Africa
African Suite
Hotel Ivoire
Frederick Douglass and the Slave Breaker
Memorial Wreath
The Southern Road
Roses and Revolutions
Legacy: My South
Blood Precious Blood
A Leader of the People
A Different Image
Ancestors
Bag Woman
The Aging Whore
Augury for an Infant

V. Me

    One Liners

    Vacant Lot

    Ghetto Girls

    Happiness

    Poet

    Verse Forms

    Birth of the Sun

    Killing a Bug

    I Like a Ravaged Face

    Women and Poets

    To the Mercy Killers

    After the Killing

    Primitives

    Beasts

    Courage: A Revolutionary Poem

    A Poet Is Not a Jukebox

    When I Think of Russia

    Detroit Renaissance

APPENDIX 2: A CAPSULE COURSE
IN BLACK POETRY WRITING:
DUDLEY RANDALL

Prologue

What is a poet?

A poet is one who writes poetry.

Why do you want to be a poet? To become famous and
   appear on TV?

Then rob a bank. You'll be on the six o'clock news.

To make money?

Go into business. It's a surer way.

To effect social change?

Become a politician.

Poets write because they must. Because they have an inner drive. Whether or not anyone hears of them, whether or not they make a cent, whether or not they affect a single person, poets write and will continue to write.

Poets' medium is language. Do you love words? The sound of them, the rhythm of them, their differences and similarities, the way they paint pictures, stir emotions? If you were a prisoner and wrote a letter, would you say, "I'm incarcerated," or would you say, "I'm in jail"? If you would say, "I'm in jail," then you are sensitive to words, and may be a poet. Read on.

The New Preparation

Often one meets people who say, "When I have five minutes I sit down and dash off a poem." One would not employ a surgeon or a house builder who says, "When I have five minutes I take a whatcha-call-em and dash off an operation or throw together a house." Each has undergone long and careful training so he can perform a skilled operation. Likewise, a poet should have intensive knowledge and practice of his art.

James Weldon Johnson in his *Book of American Negro Spirituals* reports that the persons who were most esteemed by the folk as leaders of folk singing were not necessarily those with the "best" voices. Often their voices were old and cracked, but these leaders had enormous knowledge of many folk songs. They had a vast repertory of lines and phrases and could always think of a verse to fit a particular occasion.

Likewise, Alex Haley, in his book *Roots,* which tells of how he retraced his ancestors back to a Mandingo village, reveals how the griots had a vast memory of events and people going back hundreds of years. Even if these people did not have "book learning," they had learning. Poets also are part of a long tradition, which you should learn, either orally or in books.

Formerly, Black American poets were limited to what they learned in school. They learned about Whitman, Dickinson, Eliot, Pound, Williams, Shakespeare, Keats, Shelley, and Auden. But they learned little about their heritage of Black poetry. Or, if they learned, they had to learn it on their own. Now, with the flowering of Black Studies courses and Black publishers, they have greater access to their own sources of poetry.

You can learn about Black folk poetry in such books as James Weldon Johnson's *Book of American Negro Spirituals* or Talley's *Negro Folk Rhymes* and about both folk and literary Black poetry in Sterling Brown's *Negro Caravan,* Dudley Randall's *The Black Poets,* and Xavier Nicholas's *The Poetry of Soul* and *Poetry of the Blues.*

There are many anthologies of Black poetry. Among them are LeRoi Jones and Larry Neal's *Black Fire,* Arnold Adoff's *The Poetry of Black America,* Richard Long and Eugenia Collier's *Black Poetry in America.* Poets should study the history of their literature in Saunders Redding's *To Make a Poet Black,* Sterling Brown's *American Negro Poetry,* Roger Whitlow's *Black American Literature,* and Charles P. Davis's *From the Dark Tower.*

You should read thoughtful books like W. E. B. Du Bois's *The Soul of Black Folk,* Frantz Fanon's *Black Faces, White Masks* and *The Wretched of the Earth.*

Black poets should learn the background of their history by reading Chancellor Williams's *The Destruction of Black Civilization* and the books of Joel A. Rodgers, Ben Jochannon, and Chiek Anta Diop. Stephen Henderson has a description of the unique qualities of Black poetry in his *Understanding the New Black Poetry*. Don Lee writes of the younger poets in *Dynamite Voices: Black Poets of the 1960's*. Bernard Bell reveals similarities in folk and literary poetry in *The Folk Roots of Afro-American Poetry*.

You can also learn about Black poetry not only in books, but by listening to the talk you hear all around you in the street, in the home, in bars, churches, from preachers, old folks, children, adolescents, men in varied trades and professions. All these are sources of living speech, which the poet hears and remembers and turns into poetry.

You should listen to music, all types of music, including in addition to classical music such folk music as blues, spirituals, ballads, gospel songs, children's and vendors' chants. As well as suggesting sound effects to incorporate into your poetry, they can suggest structure, mood, and tone, which you can use in your poems.

Special study should be given to Black folk poetry, for it is characterized by compression, directness, simplicity, clarity, and striking images which help to make strong poetry.

Study of a foreign literature will broaden you and give you a perspective on poetry written in your own language. In short, you should open yourself to all of life, to all experiences, to all of mankind, to the whole rich bustling wonderful world, which you will transmute into poetry.

Aims

I suppose by "Aims" is meant what you intend to do with your poetry, or the effect you wish your poetry to have on your audience. To answer these questions requires introspection, self-examination, as I suggest in my "Prologue." You may write poetry for a variety of reasons; you may wish to influence your audience in various ways. Fame, wealth, notoriety, power, I consider as insufficient motivations for writing poetry. The best motivation for writing poetry, I believe, is that something inside you, some demon, some possession, compels you to write. My happiest moments have been those in which I was writing. Yet writing is something more than therapy, self-gratification. When a poet publishes his work, he expects it to do something for his readers.

This brings up the question of ideology, or teaching. The poet's own experiences, I think, will determine how overtly didactic he will be. I can understand how a South African poet, for instance, escaping from that oppressive regime, will write of nothing but the need for liberation. In my own case, however, I was a preacher's son, and heard too much preaching at home. I believe that readers instinctively resist a writer who has an obvious design on them, who too obviously tries to manipulate them. The salesman knocks on our door with his sample case in his hand, and we immediately think of excuses not to buy . . .

However, if a poet is moved, not by a narcissistic desire to appear on television, but by some powerful experience, he may wish to share it with others. One virtue of poetry is that it makes us more alive, more perceptive, wakes up our sleeping senses. Reading Margaret Danner's poetry, for instance, with its discrimination of different textures, awakes us to a keener sensitivity to the world around us. She wrote a poem comparing carnations to gardenias, calling one masculine and the other feminine because of their texture. We had formerly confused, confounded the two flowers as just white and round, but her subtle discrimination makes us look more closely at these flowers and see their differences. She makes us more alive to the world around us.

The press of business and the tendency to abstract keeps us from really seeing the world, makes us reduce it to clichéd abstractions. We see a white man, a Negro, a Jew, a woman. Instantly there springs to mind some abstract stereotype, instead of our scrutinizing the person and trying to understand a unique individual different from all the three billion other individuals on earth. This is the virtue of poetry, that it goes back to the primitive radical roots of language, and makes us live in the poem, not move abstract counters, such as honkie, nigger, Jew, broad. If we could feel how even a pin prick hurts, then we would not be so apt to consign whole populations to death: "the final solution," "drive them into the sea," "the yellow peril," "put the nigger in his place," "the only good Indian is a dead Indian."

This is not to say that the poet should not have beliefs or ideology, but that he should not bully the reader with them. If the reader likes and respects the poet, he will unconsciously absorb his attitudes, especially if they are couched in memorable language. Poetry delights, and through delight it moves to wisdom as someone has said before.

This delight is one of the most important, though often unconscious, aims of poetry. We live on earth not knowing why we are here, where we came from or where we are going. In our brief stay we feel joy, sorrow, pain, hope and fear. The poet takes this mystery, these varied emotions, and puts them into a form which gives us

Joy and delight, joy and delight, poems
conceived in joy, endowing the world and time
with joy and delight, joy and delight, for ever.

Subject Matter

"Nothing human is alien to me." I believe that is sufficient.

Method

Method could mean many things, the manner of writing, or how to get ideas, or how to sell your work. I have decided to write here about how to market your work, for most writers want to communicate to others, and in order to communicate their work must be sold, or at least accepted, and then distributed.

A common mistake is to send your work to publications which do not use that type of work. Broadside Press, for instance, is interested in poetry, but we receive many novels, plays, and sometimes Ph.D. dissertations on such subjects as "Black In-Migration into Dorset County between 1910 and 1920." Of course such submissions are promptly returned. This waste of time could have been avoided if the writers had studied the publications of Broadside Press and learned what we customarily publish.

It's a good idea to go to your bookstore, drugstore, or public library and check their magazines. Find out which ones publish poetry. Study more than one issue of those which publish poetry, and learn what kind of poetry they publish. Do they publish poetry by Blacks; poetry in traditional forms such as sonnets, ballades, villanelles, rondeauz, rondels, triolets, canzoni, haiku, cinquaims, blank verse; experimental poetry; free verse; concrete poetry? When you find magazines which publish verse similar to the kind you write, then submit your work to those publications.

There are many publications which publish poetry. One can find them listed in *Directory of Small Presses and Magazines, Writer's Market, Writer's Digest, The Writer, Writers' Handbook.* Dudley Randall's *The Black Poets* has an appendix listing periodicals which publish Black poetry.

Don't compromise yourself by trying to slant your work toward a particular magazine. Write as well as you can in the manner which is natural to you, then submit your work to the magazines which publish that type of work.

In submitting your work, bear in mind that you will be competing against hundreds of other writers, many of whom are professionals. It's elementary that your work should be neatly typed, not mimeographed or xeroxed, one poem to a page, correctly spelled, in good grammar, with your name and address on each page, and accompanied by a stamped, self-addressed return envelope. If you don't supply envelope and return postage, the editor has no obligation to return your work.

Don't betray your amateur status by asking about copyright. You can learn about copyright by research at your public library, or by writing the Copyright Office, Washington, D.C. 20504, for free pamphlets on literary copyright. Don't appear to be a kook or a paranoiac by hinting that someone will steal your material. If you believe that, don't send it out.

A letter of transmittal is not necessary. If you must send one, make it brief and to the point. Letters may subliminally turn the editor against your work, especially if you can't spell or don't know the difference between *to* and *too, lie* and *lay, who's* and *whose, its* and *it's, lend* and *loan, there* and *their.* My heart always sinks when I receive a letter from a prisoner who says, "I'm incarcerated" instead of "I'm in jail." His diction reveals he doesn't know the principle of economy, and uses swollen language.

If you've made some of the mistakes listed above, your work will be returned to you almost immediately. If you have heard nothing about your work for three months, send the editor a letter with a return envelope requesting the return of your material unless he has decided to publish it. In most cases this will ensure its prompt return.

Most small magazines have insufficient staff to read the large number of poems they receive. There are only a few good poems and many bad ones, and on these it isn't hard to make a decision. There are, however, poems of middling quality about which the editor has doubts and which he may hold in order to make a decision. A letter requesting their return will probably tip his mind to a decision to return them.

One thing you should never do, if you are considerate, is to request that an editor comment on your poems. To do so is to confuse an editor with a teacher. The job of an editor is to select poems for his magazine, not to teach people how to write. He receives hundreds of poems and in order to report on them as promptly as possible he encloses a politely worded rejection slip. That is all the professional writer requires. He knows his poem is not accepted by magazine A and he promptly sends it to magazine B. If the editor had to explain why he rejected each poem, it would take much more of his limited time, and writers would receive reports on their work much later than they do now. There are many places where writers can obtain comments on their work. They can enroll in creative writing classes, they can take correspondence courses, they can organize or join local writers' workshops, they can attend writers' conferences. It is there, and not from editors, that they should ask for comments on their work.

The question arises whether a poet should first try to publish single poems or should wait until he has a book ready for publication. I think that a poet should first send out single poems, or groups of two or three poems, for publication first. In that way he learns about the markets for poetry, acquires experience by perhaps making some of the mistakes listed above and learning from them, and if his poems are published, he brings them to the attention of the public and of editors. If he outgrows his poems, they will have been published only in ephemeral publications like magazines, and will not be permanently exposed in books. I know several poets who published books prematurely, and they were embarrassed by them later.

To keep track of your poems, keep a notebook and record where and when you send each poem and what happens to it. Here is an example:

Title	Sent	Date	Fate	Date	Published	Price	Next
"Love"	BLACK WORLD	5/10/72	Returned				Jrnl of Blk Poetry
"Love"	Jrnl of Blk Poetry	7/13/72	Accepted	8/23/72	1/15/73	$0	ESSENCE

Notice, in the above form, you decide where next to send the poem in the event it's returned. This insures that you always have something in the mail and keeps you from feeling depressed, for as soon as a poem is returned you mail it out and always have something to hope for.

When a poem is published, enter it on a 3x5 card to keep your bibliography up to date. In the event you need to write a resume or list your published works, you will have a complete, accurate file of your published works. Example:

Jones, Ray—Bibliography—Poems
"Love (poem) JOURNAL OF BLACK POETRY, Vol 1, No. 15. Winter 1973. page 72.

The Hard Flower

Miss Brooks's title for this section seems paradoxical. Flowers are soft, not hard. I take it to mean, however, that your finished product will have the beauty of a flower, but will also have the capacity to endure, like brass or marble.*

How do you make your poems endure? Or, in other words, how do you keep them alive in the mouths of men? Naturally, men will repeat words whose meaning is important to them. Therefore, you must infuse your words with meaning. But that depends on the quality of your mind. In this context, we are speaking not of the quality of your mind, but of the technical means of causing men to remember and repeat your words. Men will repeat and remember words if they are arranged in a way which makes it easy for them to remember and repeat the words. In this context, languages differ. Let us compare English with Latin:

Boy loves girl.
Puer amat puellamn.

Both sentences mean the same thing. But reverse them.

Girl loves boy.
Puellam amat puer.

Here, the sentences have different meanings. The Latin still means the same thing—Boy loves girl—whereas in the English sentence the action is reversed. That is because of the different genius of the English and Latin languages, which gives them different capabilities. Latin is an inflected language. The meaning and relationship of words change with the inflections of the words. English, except for the plural and the possessive (girls, girl's, girls'), is an uninflected language. Changes in the meaning and relationships of words are indicated by their position in the sentence, not by changes in the word. The normal,

---

* Editor's note: means that the Black poem will be beautiful as a flower is beautiful, but will have a spine of Black strength.

idiomatic order of words in an English sentence is subject, verb, object: Boy loves girl. Therefore, English-speaking people will remember and repeat such an arrangement of words most naturally and easily. Many memorable lines have been composed in that arrangement: "We bake de bread, / They give us de crust"; "Ripeness is all"; "(He) drank his blood and ate his heart."

If you want your lines to be remembered, arrange the words in the normal, idiomatic manner of the English language—subject, verb, object—Boy loves girl. Then people will find them easy to repeat and remember. Do not write long involved sentences which confuse and puzzle the reader. You weaken your style in this way. A good model to study and learn from is the Negro secular song included in the autobiography of Frederick Douglass and reprinted in *The Negro Caravan* and *The Black Poets*: "We bake de bread, / They give us de crust."

In Latin, on the other hand, words can be shifted with great flexibility, since it is their endings, not their position in the sentence, which determine their relationships with other words. The two most conspicuous positions in a sentence are the beginning and the end. In poetry, where each sentence may be divided into separate lines, there are additional conspicuous positions, the beginning and the end of each *line*. Because of the flexibility of the Latin language, a Latin poet could compose his poem like a mosaic, placing a word here, a word there, like a red or a blue tile, according to the effect he wanted to achieve. If he wanted to emphasize the girl, he could say, *Puellam* amat puer. If he wanted to emphasize the boy, he could say *Puer* amat puellam. He could also secure emphasis by varying the last word in the sentence.

A writer in English is much more restricted in that regard. He can obtain emphasis by varying the normal word order, but he may be called inept, old-fashioned, archaic, literary, or Latinate. He must be sure the reversal is for expressiveness, not to satisfy the exigencies of meter or rime. In "The Southern Road" I began a line with "Love you I must." Margaret Danner objected to the inversion. I explained that I wanted to emphasize the love, but she insisted that I keep the natural word order. So I changed it "I have to love you." I don't know whether I gained or lost by the change. One must weigh surprise, expressiveness, and force against being natural.

Since the beginning is a prominent position, the title of a poem is important. Calling a poem "Untitled" is a lazy cop-out. A title is a handle to a poem. Often poems called "Untitled" are identified by their first line, or a line or a phrase taken from the body of the poem. The author could have identified the poem in the first place. Sometimes the meaning or explanation of a poem will depend on the title. Often we can look at the Contents of a book of poems and apprehend the essence of the book. The titles may reflect nature, or places, or people, or history. A table of contents with titles about blackness or revolution will suggest the character of the book. The poetic quality of the titles suggests the quality of the poems. Think of the titles of the Spirituals, some poetic, some dramatic: "Deep River"; "Sometimes I Feel Like a Motherless Child"; "Gamblin' Man Get Off Your Knees"; "Joshua Fit the Battle of Jericho."

You should avoid telling the reader what form the poem is, like entitling it "Sonnet," which hints that the reader doesn't know what a sonnet is. The poet should let the reader discover that the poem is a sonnet or a ballade, or, if the reader doesn't know what a sonnet or a ballade is, the poet should let the form work its peculiar magic on the reader. For that reason, I didn't call "The Southern Road" "Ballade of the Southern Road." As far as I know, no critic, book reviewer, or poet has noticed that the poem is a ballade, but I think nevertheless the form works its unique effect upon the reader.

Likewise, first lines are important. They lead the reader into the poem. They may hook his interest and stimulate him to read further, or turn him away from the poem. A critic renewed interest in Walt Whitman by writing an essay composed of quotations of his striking initial lines and other lines of beauty or power. If a book has an index of first lines, you can get an idea of the quality of the poetry by scanning the lines, and you may be attracted to a poem by its beautiful first line. First lines may be personal and dramatic: "For Godsake hold your tongue and let me love." Or imaginative: "I saw eternity the other night." Or challenging: "If we must die, let us not die like hogs." Or boldly contrasting: "First fight, then fiddle." Or strikingly rhythmic: "Out of the cradle endlessly rocking." There are countless ways to entice the reader into the poem with a striking first line.

Just as the beginning of a poem is conspicuous, the end of a poem is important. It's the last impression a reader has of a poem, and it should leave a memorable one. David Diop has some memorable last lines. The whole force of the poem seems concentrated in them. Read his poems and study his concluding lines, like these:

Oh I am lonely so lonely here. "The Renegade"
The bitter taste of liberty. "Africa"
Rise up and shout: NO! "Defiance Against Force"

In addition to writing striking and memorable titles, first lines, and con-cluding lines, make every line between the first and the last lines as good as they are, and you'll have it made.

This brings up the question of what a good line of poetry is, and how you write a good line. If we all knew what a good line of poetry is, and were able to write them, we'd all be great poets. First of all, if we live with great lines of poetry, read them, think about them, repeat them to ourselves, we may be able to absorb some of their power, and set it forth in our own writings. People who read the Bible, who know the Bible, who ponder it and try to live by it, often attain a beauty of expression. That is because the Bible is a great piece of litera-ture as well as a great religious work. Many people who were not well educated and who knew few books beyond the Bible, yet were able to speak and write with eloquence because they had absorbed some of the beauty of that Book. Think of the songs of the slave singers.

You can absorb something from the world's great poetry. Genius is not restricted to any nation or any race. Read English, Swahili, Latin, Russian, Greek, Arabic, Chinese, French, Spanish, Italian, any language which your liking, curiosity, or circumstances permits you to learn. Remember their great lines of poetry, repeat them to yourself, apply them to your daily living, and use them as touchstones to judge your lines and the lines of others you may read.

The question still arises: How do you know a good line? A good line is one which you remember without trying, whose phrasing is inevitable. What it says is said so well that there is no other way to say it better. One thing that makes it easy to remember is for it to be in the natural idiom and word order of the language: in English, in the word order of subject, verb, object, or, Boy loves girl. Analyze any good line of poetry and you will see that its syntax is clear; you don't have to worry about what the subject, or the verb, or the object is. You know what they are without having to puzzle over them. In addition, what is said is memorable, is worthwhile. By negative definition, lines like

a
the
in
to

are not memorable. What comfort or knowledge or inspiration or enjoyment can you get from lines like these? How can you remember lines like these? Yet some poets write such lines and call them lines of poetry. Such lines do not even have rhythm, since they are composed of solitary unaccented syllables. One of the prime requisites of poetry is sound, since poetry is a vocal not a visual art, and one of the components of the ordered sound of poetry is rhythm. In order to have rhythm, there must be a basis of comparison. One sound does not make rhythm, for there is nothing to compare it to. The heart beats once. No rhythm. It beats again, there is rhythm. We can say it beats fast or slowly because we can compare one beat to another. Moreover, when the poets read such lines aloud, they do not read them as distinct separate lines, but run them into the other lines. Since they run them into the other lines, they should have been run into the other lines on the page, as poetry should be written down to indicate the way it sounds, not for the way it looks upon the page. We must learn to notate our poems correctly. Unless we learn to notate our poems correctly, the reader will have no way of knowing how they should be read.

We can discern two principles by which things are remembered, contrast and similarity. In a crowd, you remember a pair of twins, dressed alike, the same age, height, weight. You also remember a strikingly dissimilar pair, like a giant and a dwarf. Likewise, we remember lines of poetry by their contrast: "Fools rush in where angels fear to tread" where the contrast is between fools and angels, rush in and fear to tread. Or we remember the similarity (repetition) of "Black love is black wealth."

Sometimes there is a combination of contrast and similarity, as in: "First fight, then fiddle" where there is contrast between fight and fiddle, which is heightened by the similarity of the alliteration of the *f*'s. The same combination of contrast and similarity is seen in "*k*ill with *k*indness."

Sometimes lines are remembered just for their human emotional qualities, as the tenderness of "I will be more / Having known your love" or the kindliness of "and kept each other warm" or the menace of "will the machine gunners please step forward" although here there is the latent contrast of the deadliness of the machine gunners and the politeness of the word "please."

It would be helpful to read poems which you admire, to notice which lines remain in your memory, analyze them to see why you remember them, repeat them, live with them, and use them as touchstones for judging others' lines and your own lines. Gradually, just as the beauty of the Bible pervades the language of those who read it frequently, the beauty of those touchstone lines which you remember will creep into the lines you write.

For an example of how to use lines as touchstones to judge poetry, to sharpen your critical faculties, and to revise your poems, compare one of the lines quoted (For Godsake hold your tongue, and let me love) with another line quoted (a).

The first line uses normal idiomatic word order (subject, verb, object: boy loves girl): hold your tongue . . . let me love, which makes the line easy to understand and to remember. The music reinforces the sense because the cadence is rapid and the guttural alliterations Godsa*k*e . . . tongue and the liquid alliterations *l*et me *l*ove harmonize with the different demands. The contrast between "shut up" and "love" also makes the line memorable. On the other hand, the second line (a) has no meaning, and is vague, vapid, vacant, and valueless. You should strike out the line "a" or place the "a" where it belongs, with its noun. This is an extreme comparison, but such testing of lines will sharpen your critical faculties and enable you to spot weaknesses in your poetry and revise them.

It is not only the meaning or syntactical form of lines that makes them memorable, but also the sound, since poetry is a vocal art.

English poetry is patterned by rhythm, measured by stressed and unstressed syllables. Quantity, or duration of sounds, is also used, especially by black poets (We a baddDDD people) but not in regular patterns. Metrists could describe many different rhythms of stressed and unstressed syllables, but the basic rhythms are iambic, trochaic, anapestic, and dactylic. Iambic rhythm consists of one unstressed syllable followed by one stressed syllable, as in "before." This is called one iambic foot. Rhythmical units are called feet from the fact that the earliest poetry was combined with music and dance. (In Africa, even today, music, poetry, and dance go together.) The line can be lengthened by adding additional feet, making the length two, three, four, five, or even eight feet. Generally, after eight feet, the line is shortened by splitting it into shorter lines.

Before / the smile / of day

is a line of three iambic feet.

Trochaic rhythm is iambic rhythm reversed, one accented syllable followed by one unaccented syllable.

After / twilight / laughter

This is a line of three trochaic feet.

Anapestic rhythm is two unaccented syllables followed by one accented syllable. Since English has many particles—unaccented monosyllables like articles (a, an, the) and prepositions (to, of, in, for, etc.) these particles are often joined with nouns or adjectives to compose anapestic feet.

At the beau / tiful smile / of the day

This is a line of three anapestic feet.

Dactyllic rhythm is the opposite of anapestic rhythm. It consists of one accented syllable followed by two unaccented syllables:

Beautiful / mystery
Wonderful / history

Each of these lines contains two dactyllic feet. Notice the different emotional effects of the different rhythms.

There is one more rhythm, the spondaic, but it is not used throughout complete poems. It consists of two accented syllables:

Fáts Dómino

Since there are almost no English words with two consecutive accented syllables, spondees are used only sporadically. They occur when a monosyllable and the accented syllable of a longer word are juxtaposed, as above, or when two monosyllables occur together:

Which hints the whole by showing the párt clear

To get the feel of the various rhythms, write poems in each rhythm, first with lines of one foot, then with lines of two, three, four, five and six feet in each line. Then you can combine rhythms. The line previously quoted, "Out of the cradle endlessly rocking," uses alternate dactylic and trochaic feet. In your practice poems, do not let the necessity of riming or of maintaining rhythm force you to alter the natural idiomatic order of words to use words which don't make sense or which don't precisely express your meaning. It's the mark of a true poet that he can compose words in a beautiful and memorable form and still make them appear artless, spontaneous, and natural.

Free verse, which is used widely today, is verse without regular patterns of rhythm or rime. This does not mean that a contemporary poet must dispense with rhythm or rime. He can use them in his free forms to suggest the meaning. He can emphasize ideas by introducing pattern, as when Etheridge Knight emphasizes two lines in his free verse poem "Hard Rock Returns to Prison" by using rime:

And then the jewel of a myth that hard Rock had once
   bit
A screw on the thumb and poisoned with syphilitic
   spit.

Those poets who ridicule traditional verse by saying it goes monotonously "da-dum, da-dum, da-dum" either have wooden ears or do not know how to read aloud. Because of the different weight of vowels and the easy-to-pronounce and hard-to-pronounce combinations of consonants in the English language, there are immense variations in the speed, quantity, tone color, and pitch of lines, to say nothing of the variations in volume, pitch, pause, tempo dictated by meaning. The "da-dum" is only an understood pattern, like the 4/4 beat in music, against which you can play innumerable variations. The best writers of free verse are those skilled in traditional verse, but many writers write bad free verse because they never learned to write traditional verse.

Poetry Today

My view of poetry today is optimistic. Not only are poets scattered over the whole country, instead of being concentrated in Chicago or New York, but they are constantly moving, teaching and learning in new places. Stephany moved from Chicago to Berkeley to Chicago, Baraka from New York to San Francisco to Newark, Margaret Danner from Chicago to Detroit to Richmond to Memphis to Chicago, Ishmael Reed from Buffalo to Berkeley. Also, the poets are stretching and growing. In their recent books Hayden, Madhubuti, Baraka, Brooks showed change and growth. Because of the emergence of Black bookstores and publishers, poets no longer have to depend on Random House or Morrow to be published. The older poets like Hayden, Brooks, Walker, and Sterling Brown are still producing, and act as guides and inspiration for younger poets.

In my own poetry, I no longer strive for the intricate, sonorous stanzas of "The Southern Road." I try for a looser form, a more colloquial diction, as in "Frederick Douglass and the Slave Breaker." I want my poems to be read and understood by children, students, farmers, factory workers, professors. I seek directness and lucidity, but also a richness so that the reader will find added meanings on each new reading. I avoid eccentricities and grotesqueries. P. J. Conkwright speaking on typography in *Scholarly Publishing*, 1972, has said what I feel about the content of typography:

> Looking back now on those Excelsior Press days (from the advantage of time and distance) I know that when I chose the fancy Ronaldson I chose the worst body type of the three before me. It was the worst because it had the most distractions in it. The little spur serifs constantly reminded the reader: "Look how elegant I am." It was what Elmer Adler used to call a "mannered" type. By "mannered" he meant that the type showed eccentric peculiarities that detracted from thought conveyance. It had mannerisms—like eye twitching, or stuttering, or elaborate gesturing. It's almost axiomatic that a good, readable type is an invisible type. Invisible in the sense that it never conspicuously makes its presence known. It's not too lean and not too fat. It has no mannerisms. It's invisible.

I said almost the same thing in my poem "Aim," in *More to Remember:* "Bodied in words transparent as the air, Which hint the whole by showing the part clear."

SELECTED BIBLIOGRAPHY

SELECTED WORKS BY DUDLEY RANDALL

A Litany of Friends: New and Selected Poems. Detroit: Lotus, 1981.

After the Killing. Chicago: Third World, 1973.

"An Answer to Lerone Bennett's Questionnaire." *Negro Digest* 7, no. 3 (1968): 41–42.

"Aphorisms." *Negro Digest* 11, no. 11 (September 1962): 45.

"Ballad of Birmingham." Broadside no. 1, *Broadside Series,* 1965.

"Ballad of Birmingham." *Correspondence,* Fall 1963.

"The Black Aesthetic in the Thirties, Forties, and Fifties." In *The Black Aesthetic,* edited by Addison Gayle Jr., 235–45. Garden City, NY: Doubleday, 1971.

"Black Emotion and Experience: The Literature for Understanding." *American Libraries* 4, no. 2 (1972): 86–90.

"Black Magic." *Ebony* 32 (August 1977): 30.

Black Poetry. Detroit: Broadside, 1969.

"Black Poet, White Critic." *Negro Digest* 14, no. 11 (1965): 4.

The Black Poets. New York: Bantam, 1971.

"Black Power." *Negro Digest* 16, no. 1 (1966): 95–96.

"Black Publisher, Black Writer: An Answer." *Black World* 24, no. 5 (1975): 32–37.

"Black Writers' Views on Literary Lions and Values." Interview. *Negro Digest* 17, no. 3 (1968): 42, 89.

"Booker T. and W. E. B." *Midwest Journal* 5, no. 1 (1952): 77–78.

Broadside Memories: Poets I Have Known. Detroit: Broadside, 1975.

"Broadside Press: A Personal Chronicle." *Black Academy Review* 1, no. 1 (1970): 40–48.

The Broadside Series. Detroit: Broadside, 1965–77.

A Capsule Course in Black Poetry Writing. With Gwendolyn Brooks, Haki R. Madhubuti, and Keorapetse Kgositsile. Detroit: Broadside, 1975.

Cities Burning. Detroit: Broadside, 1968.

"The Creative Arts." In *Black Expression: Essays by and about Black Americans,* edited by Addison Gayle Jr., 75–92. New York: Weybright and Talley, 1969.

"Cup for the Loser." *Negro History Bulletin,* no. 1 (1962): 85.

"The Cut Throat." *Negro Digest* 13, no. 9 (1964): 53–56.

"Dressed All in Pink." Broadside no. 2, *Broadside Series,* 1965.

For Malcolm: Poems on the Life and Death of Malcolm X. With Margaret Burroughs. Detroit:

Broadside, 1967.

"Games." *Negro Digest* 17, no. 8 (1968): 61.

"Ghetto Girls." *Negro Digest* 16, no. 7 (1967): 25.

Homage to Hoyt. Detroit: Broadside, 1984.

"Incident on a Bus." *Negro Digest* 14, no. 10 (1965): 70–71.

Introduction to *Cat Eyes and Dead Wood,* by Melba Joyce Boyd. Highland Park, MI: Fallen Angel, 1978.

Love You. London: Paul Bremen, 1970.

"Melting Pot." *Negro Digest* 17, no. 3 (1968): 53.

"Melvin B. Tolson: Portrait of a Raconteur." *Negro Digest* 15, no. 3 (1966): 54–57.

More to Remember: Four Decades of Poetry. Chicago: Third World, 1971.

Papers. Collections of the Manuscript Division, Library of Congress, Washington, DC.

"Old Witherington." *Negro Digest* 14, no. 11 (1965): 62.

Poem Counterpoem. With Margaret Danner. Detroit: Broadside, 1966.

"A Report on the Black Arts Convention." *Negro Digest* 26, no. 10 (1966): 13–15.

Review of *Black Poetry in America,* by Blyden Jackson and Louis D. Rubin Jr. *Black World* 24, no. 1 (1974): 73–75.

Review of *The First Cities,* by Audre Lorde. *Negro Digest* 17, no. 11–12 (1968): 13.

Review of *Songs of a Blackbird,* by Carolyn Rogers. *Black World* 19, no. 10 (1970): 52, 82.

"The Rite." *Negro Digest* 13, no. 11 (1964): 59.

"The Second Annual Black Arts Convention." *Negro Digest* 17, no. 1 (1967): 42–45.

"Shoe Shine Boy: A Short Story." *Negro Digest* 15, no. 11 (1966): 53–55.

"Three Poems by Dudley Randall: 'Colonizer,' 'Continental Hotel,' and 'Slave Castle.'" *Black World* 22, no. 11 (1973): 23–25.

"To the Mercy Killers." *Negro Digest* 15, no. 11 (1966): 66.

"Ubi Sunt, Hic Sum." *Negro Digest* 14, no. 11 (1965): 73–76.

"Victoria." *Negro Digest* 15, no. 7 (1966): 64–72.

"When I Think of Russia." *Negro Digest* 16, no. 8 (1967): 74.

"White Poet, Black Critic." *Negro Digest* 14, no. 4 (1965): 47–48.

SELECTED BIBLIOGRAPHY

Andrews, William L., Frances Smith Foster, and Trudier Harris, eds. *The Oxford Companion to African America Literature.* New York: Oxford University Press, 1997.

Bailey, Leonead Pack, ed. *Broadside Authors and Artists: An Illustrated Biographical Directory.* Detroit: Broadside, 1974.

"*Black Books Bulletin* Interviews Dudley Randall." *Black Books Bulletin* 1, no. 2 (1972): 22–26.

Blackhawk, Terry. "For Dudley Randall, 1914–2000." *Michigan Quarterly Review* 40, no. 2 (2001): 313.

Blum, Howard. "In Detroit, Poet Laureate's Work Is Never Done." *New York Times,* January 29, 1984.

Boyd, Melba Joyce. *The Black Unicorn: Dudley Randall and the Broadside Press.* A documentary film, distributed by Cinema Guild, New York, 1996.

———. "Out of the Poetry Ghetto: The Life/Art Struggle of Small Black Publishing Houses." *Black Scholar* 16, no. 4 (1985): 12–24.

———. "Remembering Dudley Randall." *Against the Current* 25, no. 6 (2000): 38–39.

———. "'Roses and Revolutions,' Dudley Randall: Poet, Publisher, Critic and Champion of African American Literature Leaves a Legacy of Immeasurable Value." *Black Scholar* 31, no. 1 (2001): 28–30.

———. *Wrestling with the Muse: Dudley Randall and the Broadside Press.* New York: Columbia University Press, 2003.

Chapman, Abraham, ed. *Black Voices: An Anthology of Afro-American Literature.* New York: New American Library, 1968.

———, ed. *New Black Voices.* New York: Mentor, 1972.

Cranford, Beaufort. "New Passages." *Detroit News,* April 6, 1983.

Davis, Arthur P. "The New Poetry of Black Hate." *CLA Journal* 13, no. 4 (1970): 382–91.

———. *From the Dark Tower: Afro-American Writers, 1900–1960.* Washington, DC: Howard University Press, 1991.

Davis, Frank Marshall. "Review of *After the Killing.*" *Black World* 23, no. 11 (1974): 85.

DeRamus, Betty. "Dudley F. Randall, 1994–2000." *Detroit News,* August 15, 2000.

Emanuel, James A. Collections of the Manuscript Division, Library of Congress, Washington, DC.

Emanuel, James A., and Theodore L. Gross, eds. *Dark Symphony: Negro Literature in America.* New York: Free Press, 1968.

Fabre, Michel. *Black American Writers in France, 1840–1980.* Urbana: University of Illinois Press, 1991.

Fowlkes, Gwendolyn. "A Conversation with Dudley Randall." *Black Scholar* 6, no. 6 (1975): 87–90.

Fuller, Hoyt. "On the Conference Beat." *Negro Digest* 15, no. 5 (1966): 88–93.

Gayle, Addison, Jr., ed. *The Black Aesthetic.* Garden City, NY: Doubleday, 1972.

Georgakas, Dan. "Young Detroit Radicals, 1955–65." *URGENT Tasks,* no. 12 (1981): 89–94.

Giovanni, Nikki. Review of *Cities Burning. Negro Digest* 28, no. 11 (1968): 95–96.

Goncalves, Joe, ed. *Black Art, Black Culture.* San Francisco: Journal of Black Poetry Press, 1972.

Harris, Trudier, and Thadious M. Davis, eds. *Dictionary of Literary Biography,* Vol. 41, *Afro-American Poets since 1955.* Detroit: Gale Research, 1985.

Hatcher, John. *The Auroral Darkness: The Life and Poetry of Robert Hayden.* Oxford, UK: George Ronald, 1984.

Hayden, Robert. Papers, National Baha'i Archives, Box 5, Wilmette, Illinois.

Hayden, Robert, ed. *Kaleidoscope: Poems by Negro Poets.* New York: Harcourt, Brace, 1968.

Henderson, Stephen. *Understanding the New Black Poetry.* New York: William Morrow, 1973.

Hodges, Frenchy. "Dudley Randall and the Broadside Press." Master's thesis, Atlanta University, 1974.

Hughes, Langston. Papers. Yale University Library, New Haven, CT.

Hughes, Langston, ed. *New Negro Poets: U.S.A.* Bloomington: Indiana University Press, 1964.

Hughes, Langston, and Arna Bontemps, eds. *The Poetry of the Negro, 1746–1970.* New York: Doubleday, 1970.

Jackson, Murray. "Dudley Randall." In *Abandon Automobile: Detroit City Poetry 2001,* edited by Melba Boyd and M. L. Liebler, 86. Detroit: Wayne State University Press, 2001.

Jordan, June. Review of *After the Killing,* by Dudley Randall. *American Poetry Review* 3, no. 2 (1974): 32–34.

King, Woody, Jr., ed. *Black Spirits: A Festival of Black Poets in America.* New York: Vintage Books/Random House, 1972.

Kniffel, Leonard. "New Hall of Fame Honors Writers of African Descent." *American Libraries* 30, no. 2 (1999): 52–53.

———. "Poet in Motion." *Monthly Detroit* 7, no. 6 (1984): 160–63.

Knight, Etheridge. Papers. The Ward M. Canaday Center, University of Toledo Library, Toledo, OH.

Lane, Ronnie M., ed. *Face the Whirlwind.* Grand Rapids, MI: Pilot Press Books, 1973.

Madgett, Naomi. "Dudley Randall." In *Oxford Companion to African American Literature,* edited by William L. Andrews, Frances Smith Foster, and Trudier Harris, 620–21. New York: Oxford University Press, 1997.

Medina, Tony, and Louis Reyes Rivera. *Bum Rush the Page: A Def Poetry Jam.* New York: Three Rivers, 2001.

Melhem, D. H. *Heroism in the New Black Poetry.* Lexington: University Press of Kentucky, 1990.

Miller, Adam David, ed. *Dices or Black Bones: Black Voices of the Seventies.* Boston: Houghton Mifflin, 1970.

Miller, R. Baxter. "Endowing the World and Time: The Life and Work of Dudley Randall." In *Black American Poets between Worlds, 1940–1960,* edited by R. Baxter Miller, 77–92. Knoxville: University of Tennessee Press, 1986.

Nicholas, A. X. "A Conversation with Dudley Randall." *Black World* 21, no. 2 (1971): 26–34.

Parks, Carole A. "10th Anniversary Celebration in Detroit: The Broadside Story." *Black World* 25, no. 3 (1976): 84–90.

Patterson, Lindsay, ed. *Rock against the Wind: Black Love Poems, an Anthology.* New York: Dodd, Mead, 1973.

"Poetry: Dudley Randall Created a Haven for Writers." Editorial. *Detroit Free Press,* August 11, 2000.

Pool, Rosey E., ed. *Beyond the Blues: New Poems by American Negroes.* Kent, UK: Hand and Flower, 1962.

———, ed. *Ik Ben de Nieuwe Newer.* The Hague, Holland: Bert, Bakker, 1965.

Redding, Saunders J. "The Black Arts Movement in Negro Poetry." *American Scholar* 42, no. 2 (1973): 330–36.

Redmond, Eugene B. *Drumvoices: The Mission of Afro-American Poetry: A Critical History.* Anchor, NY: Anchor-Doubleday, 1976.

———. "Stridency and the Sword: Literary and Cultural Emphasis in Afro-American Magazines." In *The Little Magazine in America: A Modern Documentary History,* edited by Elliott Anderson and Mary Kinzie, 33–48. New York: Pushcart, 1978.

Strong, Carline Williams. *Margaret Taylor Goss Burroughs: Educator, Artist, Author, Founder, and Civic Leader.* Ann Arbor, MI: UMI Dissertation Services, 1996.

Thompson, Heather Ann. *Whose Detroit? Politics, Labor and Race in a Modern American City.* Ithaca, NY: Cornell University Press, 2001.

Thompson, Julius E. *Dudley Randall, Broadside Press, and the Black Arts Movement in Detroit, 1960–1995.* Jefferson, NC, and London: McFarland, 1999.

Tolson, Melvin B. Collections of the Manuscript Division, Box 1, 1965–1966, Library of Congress, Washington, DC.

Turner, Darwin T., ed. *Black American Literature Poetry.* Columbus, OH: Charles E. Merrill, 1969.

Tysh, George. "A Poet Passes." *Metro Times,* August 9, 2000.

Welburn, Ron. Review of *Cities Burning,* by Dudley Randall. *Negro Digest* 19, no. 2 (1969): 94.